AS/A2 GEOGRAPHY

CONTEMPORARY CASE STUDIES

Superpowers

Cameron Dunn

Series editor: Sue Warn

Philip Allan Updates, an imprint of Hodder Education, an Hachette UK company, Market Place, Deddington, Oxfordshire OX15 0SE

Orders

Bookpoint Ltd, 130 Milton Park, Abingdon, Oxfordshire, OX14 4SB
tel: 01235 827720
fax: 01235 400454
e-mail: uk.orders@bookpoint.co.uk

Lines are open 9.00 a.m.–5.00 p.m., Monday to Saturday, with a 24-hour message answering service. You can also order through the Philip Allan Updates website: www.philipallan.co.uk

© Philip Allan Updates 2010

ISBN 978-0-34099-183-1

First printed 2010
Impression number 5 4 3 2 1
Year 2015 2014 2013 2012 2011 2010

Front cover photograph reproduced by permission of TebNad/Fotolia

Printed in Italy

Hachette Livre UK's policy is to use papers that are natural, renewable and recyclable products and made from wood grown in sustainable forests. The logging and manufacturing processes are expected to conform to the environmental regulations of the country of origin.

P01634

Contents

Introduction

Part 1: Superpower geography

Part 2: Superpower influence

Part 3: Superpowers and conflict

Part 4: Emerging powers

Part 5: China rising

Part 6: Energised India

Part 7: Declining superpowers

Part 8: Superpowers and the environment

Part 9: Examination advice

Introduction

The subject of this book is **geopolitics**. This is the branch of geography concerned with international power and politics. Modern geopolitical power and influence is closely related to economic geography and, therefore, to the processes of globalisation and development. The most powerful countries, the superpowers, are all wealthy and relatively developed nations.

The term **superpower** dates from around 1945 when the Second World War was ending and the **allied nations** were turning their minds to what sort of world they wanted when Germany and Japan were eventually defeated. The 1940s was a period of great change with some nations weakening and others gaining strength. The power and influence of nations changes over time and this often occurs at times of momentous events, such as:

■ the Industrial Revolution and the rise of the British Empire
■ the two world wars, which benefited the USA and USSR at the expense of the European nations
■ the collapse of the Berlin Wall in 1989 and the USSR in 1991, which left the USA as the only true superpower

The global power of the G8 countries in 2009

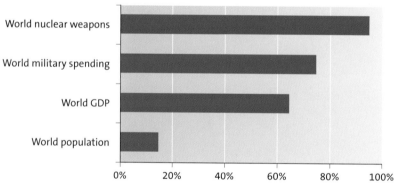

The global **recession** (the credit crunch or financial crisis), which began in late 2007, may be one of those momentous events that shifts the balance of power for good. At the moment, power and wealth is heavily concentrated in the hands of a few nations, as shown in the diagram on the left.

About this book

Part 1 begins with an examination of the historical geography of power and past superpowers. In order to understand the nature of superpowers it is useful to look back at past geographies using the benefit of hindsight. This reveals how power was maintained and projected in the past. Case studies of past empires and the growth of the EU help to build up a definition of a superpower by examining and comparing characteristics. This is then taken forward into the modern era by examining the current global balance of power.

Part 2 examines the mechanisms of superpower status in depth. Superpowers are influential globally in a number of ways. Their power is projected using a combination of cultural, economic, military and political influence. Sometimes power is used in an aggressive way — military force for instance. Usually power is wielded in 'soft' form to gain influence gradually — for example during diplomatic negotiations. Case studies based around the USA support this section.

Superpower conflict is, thankfully, surprisingly rare. Part 3 investigates examples and case studies of direct and indirect conflict where superpowers play out their conflicting world views through mechanisms like the space race or through 'third party' countries such as Sudan.

Parts 4–6 examine the **emerging powers**, particularly Brazil, Russia, India and China (the BRICs). A common view is that the world is in the process of a major shift in power from a **unipolar** world dominated by the USA to a more complex **multipolar** one where emerging powers are increasingly influential. Both China and India are gaining economic power and as **demographic superpowers** they have the potential to become major world markets.

Part 7 examines the potential 'losers' in this global power shift. Case studies of the USA and USSR illustrate the problems that can result from a loss of power and influence.

Part 8 investigates the impact of superpower growth and **resource consumption**. It assesses the degree of tension between the need for a more environmentally sustainable world and continued economic growth in China and India, as well as using the wildernesses of the Arctic and Antarctic as examples of resource-rich areas, which could prove an increasing source of tension in a world where natural resources are dwindling.

Part 9 provides guidance on assessment and examination questions including:
- using data stimulus material
- learning and using case studies
- developing essay writing skills
- using models and theories

There is a particular focus on the synoptic nature of the exams at A2.

Key terms

Allies: the military alliance that defeated Germany and Japan in the Second World War. The Allies consisted of the USA, UK, Russia and other nations.

Arms race: when two or more countries compete to have ever more powerful military forces. Arms races often occur just before major conflicts.

Biocapacity: the ability of an area, or the whole planet, to generate ongoing renewable resources and absorb wastes without being degraded.

Bipolar: a world order with two superpowers, such as the Cold War era 1945–90 when the USA and USSR were the two superpowers.

BRICs: the emerging powers, as defined by Goldman Sachs in 2001 — Brazil, Russia, India and China.

Capitalism: an economic system in which the means of production (industry) is owned by private individuals whose aim is profit. Private rights and private property are valued, and economic decisions are made by individuals and companies.

Colonial: direct rule of another country or territory by a foreign power; usually the area is conquered initially by military force.

Communism: an economic and political system in which the state owns the means of production (industry) to prevent exploitation and excessive profits, with the aim of creating an equal and classless society.

Conflict: disagreement between two or more parties. It can also refer to a situation of war or a political standoff.

Consumption: the use of goods and services, which by its very nature uses up natural resources.

Cultural assimilation: the adoption of outside cultural values; taking on board the attitudes and views of another group and in the process altering the original culture.

Cultural imperialism: promoting one culture in an attempt to reduce the influence of another. It can be overt, for instance a colonial power banning traditional cultural practices or more subtle, such as the promotion of Western consumer values by large transnational corporations (TNCs).

Culture: a set of shared values, attitudes, behavioural norms and traditions. Culture gives a group of people a cohesive, shared world view.

Demographic superpower: a country with a very large population. There are currently 11 countries with populations of over 100 million.

Dependency: an uncomfortable reliance on a narrow economic base, such as relying on the export of one or two commodities. Dependency leaves a country vulnerable to fluctuations in price and demand.

Emerging power: countries gaining in economic, military and political strength. Emerging powers are becoming more significant globally.

Failed state: a country that lacks an effective government and where the rule of law has broken down, leading to social and economic turmoil. Many are dangerous locations with limited diplomatic relations with the rest of the world.

Foreign debt: money owed by governments to other governments, banks and international lending organisations such as the World Bank and International Monetary Fund.

Foreign direct investment: money invested by TNCs in factories and offices in foreign countries.

G8: the group of eight of the world's most powerful developed countries — USA, UK, Russia, Germany, Japan, France, Italy and Canada.

G20: the G8 group of countries expanded to include the BRICs and other large regional powers, totalling 20 countries in all.

Geopolitics: the geographical patterns and processes of international power and politics.

Glocalisation: local or regional scale adaptations of global phenomena — for example, a global brand such as McDonald's adapting its menus to suit local tastes.

Hegemony: the domination of one group over another using power and influence, rather than force.

Hyperpower: a dominant superpower with no rivals, such as the position of the USA in the 1990s and early twenty-first century.

Ideology: a set of aims and ideas, especially political ones, that inform the way the world is viewed and interpreted; a set of universally accepted truths.

Intergovernmental organisations: organisations whose members are nations such as the United Nations or World Trade Organization.

Leapfrogging: development by 'jumping' over a technological stage, such as developing mobile telephones without having had a hardwired landline network.

Liberalisation: creating a free market economy by removing restrictions on trade, privatising government-owned industries and reducing state control of the economy.

Multipolar: a world in which there are many superpowers rather than one or two.

Neocolonialism: relationships between the developed and developing world, similar to the colony–imperial power relationship of the past, but which are manifest through trade, aid and debt patterns rather than by direct rule of colonies.

Outsourcing: shifting manufacturing production or services from the developed world to the developing world. When it involves the tertiary sector, this is often called 'business process outsourcing'.

Populism: a type of politics that appeals to the concerns of ordinary people, often using a 'people versus the powerful' rhetoric. It is a force in Latin American politics.

Proxy war: a war when superpowers use third party countries or groups to fight each other, rather than fighting directly. Superpowers might support opposing sides in a civil war.

Sphere of influence: the geographical area that a superpower or other power either controls or has political and economic influence over.

Superpower: a country, or grouping of countries, that has global influence and the ability to project its power globally.

Terrorism: violence and the threat of violence against civilians, rather than against armed forces. Terrorist acts aim to create fear and are seemingly random. They aim to force the acceptance of an ideology rather than win territory.

TNC: a transnational corporation is a company with operations in more than one country.

Unipolar: a world dominated by a sole superpower.

Websites

There are a number of useful websites that focus on geopolitics and superpowers. The list below shows some of the best:

- **www.dni.gov** — the USA Office of the Director of National Intelligence. It produces periodic reports on the state of the world from a geopolitical perspective, such as the *Global Trends 2025 Report* (2008) and *Vision 2015* (2008). Both reports attempt to imagine the future geopolitical world landscape.
- **www.wri.org** — the World Resources Institute is a global information portal with a large amount of up-to-date statistical information on countries and issues. It is useful for identifying economic and social trends.
- **www.weforum.org/en/index.htm** — the World Economic Forum is a foundation based in Geneva that is dedicated to bringing together global leaders in business, economics and politics. Its annual meeting in Davos is a key global event for elites.
- **www.economist.com** — the website of a weekly magazine on economics, business, politics and global issues. It is well respected and a good source of accurate news information, covered in more depth than many newspapers. The magazine was first published in 1843 and there is an excellent online archive. It supports market capitalism.
- **www.newint.org** — *New Internationalist* is a print magazine first published in 1973. Most back issues are online in an excellent archive. It is broadly anti-capitalist and makes a good foil to *The Economist*.
- **www.globalissues.org** — a website founded by Anup Shah in 1998. It is very much a personal website that covers global issues in depth. It is not neutral, but contains some interesting material that is usually referenced carefully.
- **www.chinadaily.com.cn** — the online version of the English-language print newspaper. It is a good source of information on China but beware, its owner is the Chinese Communist Party.
- **www2.goldmansachs.com** — Goldman Sachs is the US bank that coined the term 'BRICs'. The 'ideas' section of its corporate website produces periodic updates on the BRICs and other global economic issues.
- **news.bbc.co.uk** — the BBC website is undervalued in many ways. However, it archives all news stories, so you can search for just about anything and see what web pages looked like in 1997!

1 — *Using case studies*

Question

Explain who the G8 countries are and use the diagram in this introduction (p. vi) to assess their global significance.

Guidance

Make sure you produce a complete list of countries. You might want to comment on which countries are not in the G8, e.g. China and India. The figure suggests that there are differences between the G8's military, economic and demographic significance.

Superpower geography

What is a superpower?

Superpowers are nations, or groupings of nations, that have a disproportionate degree of power compared with other nations. Their power is global in nature. This means that their **sphere of influence** is, in effect, the whole world. A useful definition of a superpower is that 'a superpower must be able to conduct a global strategy…to command vast economic potential and influence and present a universal ideology' (Professor Paul Dukes, University of Aberdeen). This definition suggests that superpowers, whether modern or historical, share a number of characteristics:

- **economic wealth** — money is required to fund the construction of infrastructure, particularly the military machine that superpowers require to maintain their status. Money can be used to buy influence, for instance through foreign aid.
- **military dominance** — superpowers may not use military force often, but the threat of it is a source of power and a bargaining chip. Military power needs to be mobile and capable of reaching distant places if it is to be a truly potent threat.
- **dominant ideology** — a superpower nation usually has a set of shared core beliefs and values that are believed to be superior to the beliefs of others. This ideology provides the powerful with a justification for dominating others on the basis that their ideology is 'right'.
- **plentiful resources** — many superpower nations have large natural resources such as land, fossil fuels, mineral wealth and people. A resource base may be important in the early stages of economic development. However, once they have attained power, superpowers often begin to control and use the resources of others.

Superpower status is achieved when these characteristics reinforce each other to create a powerful global force. Figure 1.1 shows that the 'base' of superpower status is economic wealth and power. From this springs a military, cultural, ideological and geographical superstructure that reinforces superpower aspirations.

Figure 1.1
Superpower status

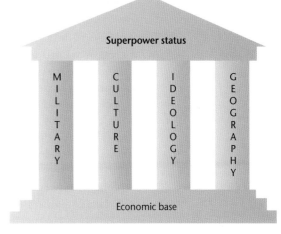

The Italian Marxist philosopher Antonio Gramsci (1891–1937) developed the concept of cultural hegemony in the 1920s. Gramsci believed that the ruling classes in a society (the bourgeoisie) maintained their power by constructing a 'hidden' consensus believed in by all people in that society. This is the concept of **hegemony**, which means a dominating force. To Gramsci, hegemony was the dominant ideology of the ruling classes which the rest of society accepted as 'the way things are' and, therefore, did not attempt to overthrow or revolt against.

In Marxist thought, this ideology is capitalism. The ruling classes own the means of production (businesses and factories) and employ workers, often for low wages. Marxists believe this system to be unfair because workers toil for little reward while the ruling class becomes rich. Gramsci was troubled by the fact that workers rarely seemed to perceive this unfairness and attempt to overthrow it.

The concept of a hegemonic ideology may help explain why workers accept capitalism. Gramsci argued that workers accepted the unfair system because they believed the system was in their best interests. The ruling class reinforced this view by:
- employment — even poorly paid employment is better than nothing
- using religion as a way of binding society together
- providing workers with basic forms of social security — just enough to 'keep a lid' on revolution

Gramsci's ideas can be extended to the influence of superpowers. Their power is partly maintained because other nations and people accept them as there seems to be no alternative. These ideas can be explored further by examining some historical examples of superpowers.

Case study 1 — ALL ROADS LEAD TO ROME

Most roads did indeed lead to Rome 1800 years ago. Rome lay at the centre of an empire that stretched across three continents from what is now Britain, to Turkey, Israel, Egypt and Morocco (Figure 1.2). The Roman Empire was the first true superpower. Its origins lay in what is now Italy around 200 BC. From this core the empire grew, by conquest, to reach its fullest extent in around AD 200. Rome's influence began to wane in about AD 400 and by AD 450 the western half of the empire had collapsed, leaving the centre of power in Constantinople (modern-day Istanbul).

Rome remained a global power centre for an extraordinarily long period — over 500 years. How was this possible? The genius of the Romans was to recognise that power could not be maintained by force alone. The Roman army and navy were both technologically advanced fighting machines but they could not police every corner of the vast empire. In order to be successful, Rome needed to exert its hegemony in ways that made conquered people 'buy in' to the Roman way of life. How the Romans did this is illustrated in a scene from the Monty Python comedy film *The Life of Brian*. In one scene, Reg, an anti-Roman revolutionary leader asks the question 'what have the Romans ever done for us?' The gathering of revolutionaries answers by reeling off numerous Roman achievements to which Reg is forced to reply 'All right, but apart from the sanitation, the medicine, education, wine, public order, irrigation, roads, a freshwater system, and public health, what have the Romans ever done for us?'.

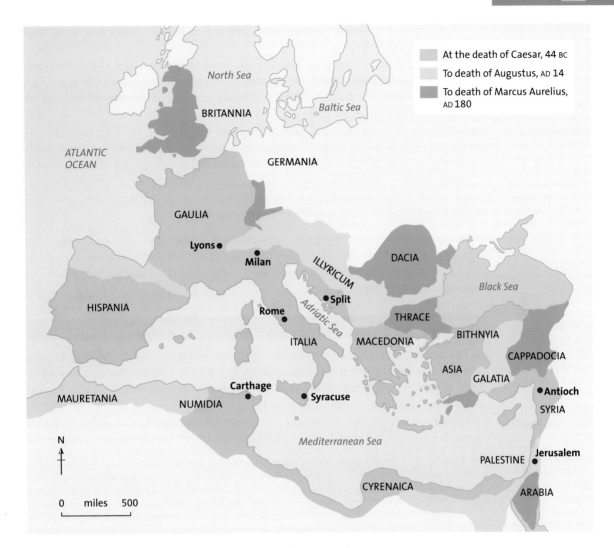

Figure 1.2
Growth of the Roman Empire to AD 180

Referring back to Figure 1.1, it is possible to examine how the Romans maintained their empire for hundreds of years:

■ **economy** — slavery was used extensively to support the economy. Up to 25% of the population were slaves, many captured as the empire expanded. This 'free' labour was a major contributor to the lavish lifestyles of wealthy Romans. Other superpowers such as the British Empire, pre-civil war USA and the USSR have made use of slave labour.

■ **military** — the Roman army was technically advanced in both strategy and equipment. Roman legions were organised hierarchically and soldiers (full citizen volunteers) were well paid and equipped. Legions were used to dominate conquered territory (see Figure 1.2) whereas the less well-equipped auxiliary troops (not full citizens) were used in a supporting role.

■ **ideology** — power and control are the key ideological characteristics of the Roman Empire. Power over conquered regions was gained by **cultural assimilation** or 'Romanisation'. Roman towns, aqueducts, temples and government buildings symbolised the civilising of barbarian peoples. Roads, armies and Roman currency demonstrated that the emperor was in control.

- **geography** — at its height, the Roman road network spanned over 50 000 miles and tied the vast empire together. It allowed rapid communication via the state mail system as well as the quick movement of armies to areas of rebellion. Roads became key economic arteries for trade.
- **culture** — art, religion, food, architecture and music were all important parts of Roman culture. Ruling elites in conquered regions could expect to live like Romans so long as they complied with the rule of Rome. The Roman palace at Fishbourne in West Sussex is thought by some to be the first-century residence of a pro-Roman British tribal chief. Some Iron Age tribal leaders submitted to Rome and were rewarded with underfloor heating, aqueducts and mosaic floors.

Interestingly, the Romans were not precious about their religion. As long as they were not seen as a threat to the state, many local deities were assimilated into the polytheistic pantheon of Roman gods. This allowed many conquered peoples to continue to worship their own gods.

Case study 2 — THE BRITISH EMPIRE

A characteristic of a superpower is an ability to invest in new technology to help maintain power. In the nineteenth century the British Empire was the innovative core of the rapidly expanding Industrial Revolution (Figure 1.3). The empire was maintained by force and the threat of force. During the period 1815–1905, Britain followed a policy of 'Pax Britannica', which literally means 'British peace'. A global Royal Navy protected trade routes and dispersed troops and arms to trouble spots.

Figure 1.3
The British Empire in 1919

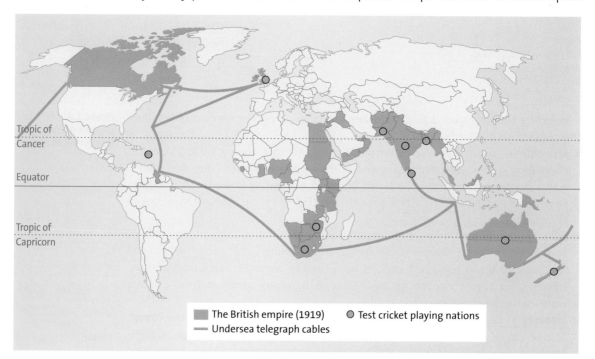

Legend:
- The British empire (1919)
- Undersea telegraph cables
- Test cricket playing nations

The navy operated the 'two-power rule', meaning that naval strength had to exceed the strength of the next two largest navies in the world. Britain ruled a unipolar world for most of the nineteenth century.

The British Empire was the first truly global superpower empire. As the empire expanded, the challenge of maintaining global connections grew. The perfection of the ocean-going steamship in the 1860s using triple expansion steam engines and screw propellers greatly assisted trade and communication but it was the international telegraph system that finally connected the empire. From the late 1850s, Britain undertook to connect its empire using undersea telegraph cables to transmit messages around the world using Morse code. The cables, weighing up to 2 tonnes per mile, were laid on the seabed from steamships. The first reliable transatlantic cable was laid in 1866. By 1872, a telegraph message could be sent from London to Australia and by 1876 to New Zealand (see Figure 1.3). The scale of the imperial telegraph system is staggering — in terms of technological innovation and cost it should perhaps be compared to the race to the Moon in the 1960s. British imperialists had created a kind of 'Victorian internet'.

2 Using case studies

Question

(a) What are the essential characteristics for superpower status?
(b) Discuss the factors that, in the past, allowed superpowers to control their spheres of influence.

Guidance

(a) The key here is that true superpowers have a number of characteristics that are sources of power, rather than just one. Military dominance, and economic and cultural power are important. A cohesive 'world view' or ideology that is projected around the world is also a vital characteristic.

(b) Bear in mind that the British Empire and Roman Empire existed long before rapid electronic communication. Nevertheless, both realised the importance of transport and communication to tie their empires together. Military power is almost always important. In Roman times, the army was key whereas naval power and reach was crucial to the British Empire. Both powers imposed their cultural values on areas they controlled.

End of empire

The Roman and British empires eventually collapsed, despite their technological sophistication and military and economic power. For Britain, it is easy to blame the Second World War for the collapse. In 1946, the UK was lent $3.5 billion by the USA, which prevented national bankruptcy (the last repayment to the USA was made in 2006) but it was clear that the UK could no longer afford its empire. Over the next 20 years most colonies were given independence.

However, the seeds of the empire's collapse were present long before 1946 as internal and external forces undermined the imperial system of government. Figure 1.4 models the collapse of imperial superpowers.

Figure 1.4
Internal and external pressures on imperial superpowers

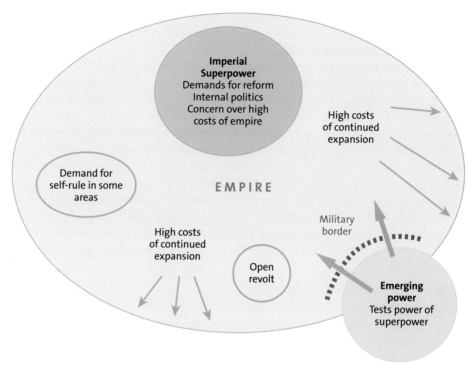

The British Empire was affected by a number of factors that undermined its stability:

■ pressure for greater independence in the 'white' colonies of Canada and Australia, followed by open revolt in India in the 1920s and 1930s

■ internal pressures at home, such as the demand for female suffrage around 1900 and public debate over the morality of the Boer Wars (1899–1902) in South Africa, and the Amritsar massacre in India in 1919

■ the rising power of the USA, Russia and Germany leading to arms races in the build up to both world wars. From 1900, Britain had to focus far greater political and economic resources on Europe compared to the Pax Britannica period

There is a built-in paradox to empire building. As empires develop and wealth increases, colonial people are exposed to the wealth, power and ideas of the imperial power and inevitably want that which they don't have. Similarly, emerging powers begin gradually to obtain the technology and ideas that originated in the imperial superpower. This can happen through trade and exchange, copying and even espionage. Emerging powers and colonial people begin to threaten the stability of the empire. Perhaps this explains why some imperial powers maintained their colonial possessions in a state of underdevelopment to prevent new economic and political ideas taking root.

The end of empire and the Cold War

Empire building ended in 1945 when the European powers began the period of decolonialisation. During the postwar period power structures have taken a different form based on international relations, rather than on the amount of land countries control.

It is important to realise the consequences of decisions made by the Allies (USSR, UK, France, USA and China) in the years just before and after the end of the Second World War. These decisions still shape the world today as most of the international organisations so important in modern-day global decision making were set up during this period (Table 1.1).

*Table 1.1
Forging the postwar world*

Date	Agreement	Parties	Decisions
1941	The Atlantic Charter	UK and USA (Winston Churchill and President Franklin Roosevelt)	Agreement to lower trade barriers, allow self-determination of people (effectively ending colonial rule), to not seek further territorial expansion and to disarm after the war
1942	Declaration of the United Nations	UK, USA, USSR and China plus 22 other countries	Agreement to unite to defeat the Axis powers (Germany, Italy and Japan) and seek a joint peace and to uphold the Atlantic Charter agreement
1944	Bretton Woods Conference	44 allied nations led by the USA and UK	Agreement to set up the International Bank for Reconstruction and Development (now the World Bank), the International Monetary Fund (IMF) and General Agreement on Tariffs and Trade (now the World Trade Organization or WTO)
1945	United Nations Conference on International Organization	50 allied nations	Agreement on the United Nations Charter
1949	North Atlantic Treaty	12 European and North America countries	Agreement to create a joint security and military alliance (NATO)

Table 1.1 illustrates how many of the organisations that are key to international geopolitics date from the 1940s. The two key Axis powers, Germany and Japan, have grown economically since 1945 but agreements set up by the Allies, as well as internal pressures, have prevented Germany and Japan from regaining significant military power. Both countries have military forces, but not nuclear weapons or large navies.

The postwar consensus did not last long. Between 1945 and 1950 the geography of Europe was reshaped as two conflicting superpower visions of the world clashed. Capitalism, in the shape of the USA, and communism, in the shape of the USSR, fought for sphere of influence hegemony in Europe. Capitalism and communism are two political and economic systems that are fundamentally opposed. The central idea of capitalism is individual ownership of wealth and property. This means that people are free to make, and lose, as much money as they like. Communism rejects this idea, based on the view that private wealth creates inequality, and instead substitutes government ownership of property. These views are so diametrically opposed that it is perhaps not surprising that the USA and USSR 'fell out' so dramatically and the world diverged quickly into a **bipolar** one (Figure 1.5). By 1950, the two Cold War superpowers were engaged in a nuclear **arms race**, which ended only with the collapse of communism in 1990.

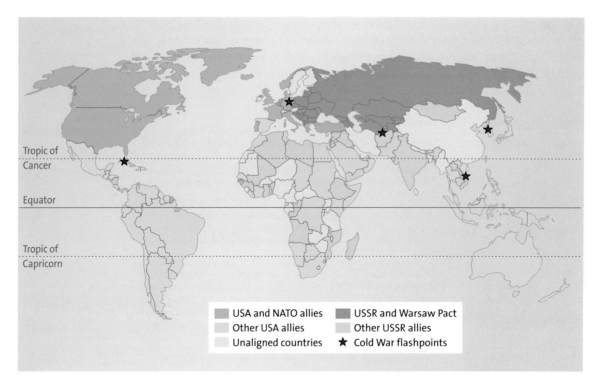

Figure 1.5
The bipolar world of the Cold War in 1980

The period 1950–90 is often referred to as the 'Cold War'. The USA and USSR super-powers had hostile relations throughout this period and both countries built up vast arsenals of nuclear weapons. However, the Cold War never became a 'hot war'. The two superpowers did come close to open conflict in 1962 when Cuba planned to station Soviet nuclear weapons on its soil, only 90 miles from the USA. Other events during this period that amounted to 'proxy' conflicts between the two superpowers include:

- the 1950–53 Korean War, when the USA supported South Korea and the USSR supported China and North Korea
- the Berlin blockade in 1948, when the USSR cut Berlin off from the rest of Germany and the USA and NATO Allies supplied the city by air
- the space race in the 1950s and 1960s
- the summer Olympic Games between 1952 and 1988
- the 1979–89 occupation of Afghanistan by the USSR; the CIA supported anti-Soviet forces

During the Cold War, the 'iron curtain' divided Europe physically and ideologically into a communist east and a capitalist west. The iron curtain referred to the physical and political border that divided Europe and which was closed to trade, migration and the exchange of ideas. In Europe, Germany was divided into two countries by the Cold War. Capitalist West Germany aligned itself with NATO and the EU; communist East Germany was a member of the Warsaw Pact. This pact was the USSR's response to NATO. Germany remained divided until reunification following the collapse of the Berlin Wall (1989) and eastern European communism in 1989–91. In Europe, the European Union (EU) created an economic grouping based on free markets and trade which was an effective counter to communist expansion in Europe.

BUILDING A SUPERPOWER: THE EU

In 2009, the EU represented the world's largest economy. The EU is an economic and political alliance of sovereign states which operates as a trade bloc (Figure 1.6). In some ways, the EU might be classed as a superpower:

■ Its economy is large, and per capita incomes are high.

■ It is a nuclear power (France and the UK) with large military resources.

■ It has a global currency, the euro, and few internal borders or barriers to prevent trade and migration.

In some ways, the EU is a federation of states in much the same way as 50 states make up the USA. In other ways, the EU lacks the coherence of a superpower:

■ Some countries, for example the UK, have opted out of policies such as the euro and a borderless state. This weakens the impact of these policies as they are not universally adopted.

■ The 27 governments of the EU differ on as many policies as they agree on.

■ The EU has yet to develop a truly joint defence and foreign policy.

It is ironic that it was Britain's wartime prime minister Winston Churchill who led moves towards European union. Speaking in 1946 he argued that the way to avoid future war

Figure 1.6
The expanding EU

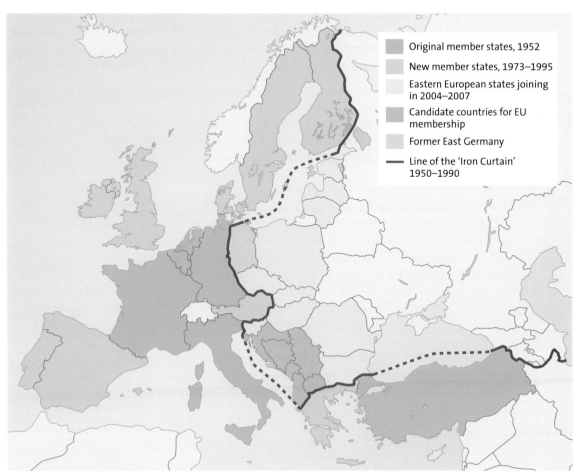

	Original member states, 1952
	New member states, 1973–1995
	Eastern European states joining in 2004–2007
	Candidate countries for EU membership
	Former East Germany
—	Line of the 'Iron Curtain' 1950–1990

in Europe was 'to re-create the European family, or as much of it as we can, and to provide it with a structure under which it can dwell in peace, in safety and in freedom. We must build a kind of United States of Europe.'

The idea that unity was a way to avoid future conflict seemed sensible, as did the idea that economic strength could be gained by working together. This was particularly the case in a Europe where the 'great powers' of the colonial era were reduced to relying on US aid under the postwar Marshall Plan just to keep the lights on. European treaties since 1951 have created an ever larger and more integrated EU:

- 1951 — Treaty of Paris creates the European Coal and Steel Community
- 1957 — Treaty of Rome creates the European Economic Community (EEC), forerunner of the EU
- 1985 — Schengen agreement to remove internal border controls within the EU
- 1986 — Single European Act allows the EEC to have a joint foreign policy
- 1992 — Maastricht Treaty formally creates the EU
- 1993 — creation of a single market with no import and export controls
- 2002 — the launch of the euro single currency

The EU has grown gradually, over a period of 50 years, to become a rival to the USA at least in terms of economic power. However, a union of 27 sovereign states is very different to one sovereign state. It is difficult to imagine the election of the EU President generating quite the same global hype as the election of President Obama in 2008. In 2004, many former Warsaw Pact countries in what had been communist eastern Europe joined the EU. This radical shift in Europe's political and economic geography might be seen as the final chapter in the story of a Europe divided by Cold War geopolitics.

Using case studies 3

Question

(a) Explain the significance of the 1940s (Table 1.1) to the world we live in today.
(b) What was the Cold War and why is 'Cold War' a somewhat misleading term?
(c) To what extent should we consider the EU a superpower?

Guidance

(a) Much of the postwar period has been about avoiding another world war. Many important institutions, which are still highly relevant today, were set up with this aim in mind. Improving economics, global finance, trade and dispute resolution explain why institutions such as the United Nations were set up. It is worth considering if some parts of this system might need updating to cope with the demands of the twenty-first century.

(b) The Cold War was a world divided into a capitalist 'west' and communist 'east' led by the USA and USSR superpowers. These powers had sharply contrasting ideologies. The term misleads to some degree because war did not occur, although various proxy conflicts and competitions took the place of all-out conflict.

(c) The EU is certainly not a classic superpower because it has built itself up over 50 years into a powerful global force. However, it remains fundamentally 27 separate nations. These nations share many characteristics but it is difficult to argue that they have a common culture and ideology. The EU has the potential to be a powerful military force if it chose to work more closely. Collectively it is the world's largest economy, much larger than the USA.

Part 2

Superpower influence

There are few colonies today other than a few small dependent islands such as St Helena, American Samoa and Martinique. Even these have elements of self-rule. During the colonial era, overseas possessions of powerful countries were subservient to their colonial masters. Colonial rule typically consisted of:

- forceful takeover of land and land rights by the colonial power, with ownership passed to the colonial government, armed forces, private companies or colonial settlers
- government by decree, with virtually no democratic process or suffrage, combined with the constant threat of force to put down rebellion
- imposition of colonial legal systems, religion and culture; sometimes the banning of indigenous cultural practices and even enslaving or genocide of indigenous peoples
- the removal of natural resources such as fossil fuels, ores, minerals and timber to support the home economy
- the conversion of land into plantations to produce cash crops to support the home economy

Today, powerful countries exert power in more subtle ways because the option of direct control has gone.

Mechanisms of power

At present, the world's largest economy is the EU, but few people would argue that it is the dominant superpower. Similarly, in 2009 Japan had the second largest economy of a nation state, just surpassing China's GDP figure of $4.8 billion, but Japan is not talked of as an emerging superpower whereas China is. This tells us that while economic power is an important factor in superpower status it is by no means the only factor.

Table 2.1 shows an index of superpower status using data from 2006–07. Seven different indicators are used ranging from gross national product to oil reserves and the global influence of spoken language. To some degree the choice of data is fairly arbitrary and other indicators might be used, although the results would be similar.

Table 2.1 *An index of superpower status*

Data for 2006–07	USA	EU	China	Russia	India	Japan	Brazil	Gulf states*
Population (millions)	300	490	1300	145	1100	128	180	35
Rank	*4*	*3*	*1*	*6*	*2*	*7*	*5*	*8*
GNP ($ trillion)	$13	$16	$3.2	$1.2	$1.1	$4	$1.3	$0.8
Rank	*2*	*1*	*4*	*6*	*7*	*3*	*5*	*8*
TNC HQs (out of global top 500)	162	163	24	4	6	67	5	1
Rank	*2*	*1*	*4*	*7*	*5*	*3*	*6*	*8*
Language (million global speakers)	510	510	1051	255	490	128	213	230
Rank	*2.5*	*2.5*	*1*	*5*	*4*	*8*	*7*	*6*
Oil reserves (billion barrels)	21	6	16	60	5	0.06	12	484
Rank	*3*	*6*	*4*	*2*	*7*	*8*	*5*	*1*
Patent filings 2006	391 000	308 000	129 000	29 000	8100	514 000	4750	304
Rank	*2*	*3*	*4*	*5*	*6*	*1*	*7*	*8*
Nuclear warheads (number)	5000+	550	400	5000++	100	–	–	–
Rank	*2*	*3*	*4*	*1*	*5*	*7*	*7*	*7*
Sum of ranks	**17.5**	**19.5**	**22**	**32**	**36**	**37**	**42**	**46**

*Gulf states are the UAE, Bahrain, Qatar, Saudi Arabia, Kuwait and Oman combined

Table 2.1 could be interpreted as showing:

■ the USA and EU as superpowers, with the USA being a **hyperpower**
■ China as the key emerging superpower
■ Russia and India as emerging powers — with strengths in some areas
■ Brazil, Japan and the Gulf states as regional powers

It is questionable whether the EU and USA are really equal in terms of power. As one nation, the USA has greater political and economic coherence than the 27 separate states of the EU. Within international bodies such as the WTO, IMF and UN, the EU usually votes as a coherent bloc, but not always. Sometimes individual national interest takes precedence over the interests of the EU as a whole.

4 Using case studies

Question

(a) **Comment on the value of the measures of superpower status shown in Table 2.1.**
(b) **Suggest some alternative measures of superpower status.**

Guidance

(a) Some measures are indicators of size, such as population, but not necessarily indicators of power. From a power perspective, nuclear arsenal size might be seen as key although there are a number of countries (e.g. Pakistan) that have nuclear weapons but few other sources of power. Oil reserves may be important, but oil can be bought on international markets. TNCs are huge generators of wealth, strongly correlated with total GNP.

(b) Other measures could include measures of development such as the Human Development Index. Linked to patent filings are royalties and licence fees which tend to accrue to the rich and powerful. Internet users and perhaps mobile phone penetration might indicate level of technology use.

International decision making

Superpowers have significant power internationally through memberships of **inter-governmental organisations**. These are key economic and political decision-making bodies, many of which were set up as part of the allied postwar consensus (see Table 1.1). Critics of these organisations see them as helping to maintain the hegemony of western capitalism and free markets at the expense of weaker countries and alternative political and economic systems. The opposing view is that these organisations serve to keep powerful nations talking and negotiating rather than fighting. Table 2.2 shows the membership of key international organisations. The data show that some countries/country groupings get to attend all of the important global meetings whereas others are much less involved. This system, essentially dating from the 1940s, is under pressure. Russia was admitted to the G7 in 1997 (now the G8) and is likely to join the OECD soon. The permanent membership of the UN Security Council may also be reformed to include Japan, Brazil, India and Egypt or perhaps a Middle Eastern state.

The G8, or Group of 8 countries, has an interesting history, which reveals changes in international power politics:

- Originally the G6 (UK, USA, Japan, France, Germany and Italy), the group formed in 1975 as an informal meeting of the leaders of western, capitalist democracies. The group's formation was largely in response to the 1973 oil crisis and the recession that followed.
- Canada joined to form the G7 in 1976 and the group pursued shared economic and political goals. All member states sat on the USA's side in the Cold War with the USSR.

Table 2.2
Membership of key international organisations

	USA	EU	Japan	Russia	China	India	Brazil	Gulf states
Member of the WTO								
United Nations Security Council seat (permanent)								
Member of G8								
OECD member country								
Member of NATO								
5%+ votes at the IMF								

- Following the collapse of the USSR, Russia joined the now G8 in 1994. This move recognised the renewed importance of Russia as an emerging capitalist power, and exporter of natural resources and nuclear power.
- By 2005 the G8 + 5 (or G13) began meeting as the G8 plus Mexico, Brazil, China, South Africa and India. This shift reflected the increasing importance of the emerging powers in trade, climate change negotiations and the world economy.

A major power shift occurred in 2008-09 at three summits (London, Washington and Pittsburg), where the global financial crisis was top of the agenda. These summits were G20 summits (the G13 plus Egypt, Saudi Arabia, Australia, Argentina, Indonesia, South Korea and Turkey). It is likely that in the future the G20 will become the key informal international decision-making forum, reflecting a fundamental shift in power towards the emerging economies, especially in Asia.

Military reach

The EU and China lack the global military reach of the USA. As a military power the USA is unrivalled as it has the ability to deploy its armed forces across the globe rapidly. Its military spending (Figure 2.1) dwarfs that of the EU and the other powers. Other powers do have long-range nuclear weapons technology in the form of intercontinental ballistic missiles (ICBMs) but none has a military presence in so many parts of the world (see Case Study 4).

Figure 2.1
Military spending
in 2008

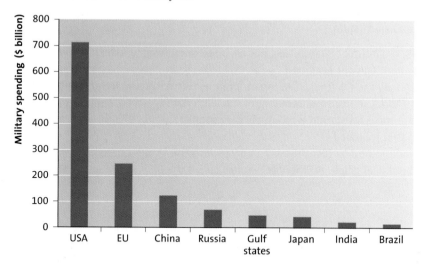

Case study 4 THE USA'S GLOBAL MILITARY NETWORK

The USA's military network is shown in Figure 2.2. The superpower has troops, aircraft and naval forces stationed across the globe, on every continent except Antarctica (where it keeps a permanently manned scientific station at the South Pole). The USA is able to project its power globally like no other nation. This alone represents a threat to nations that might threaten the security of the USA. The reasons for the global distribution of US military might are partly historical and partly modern:

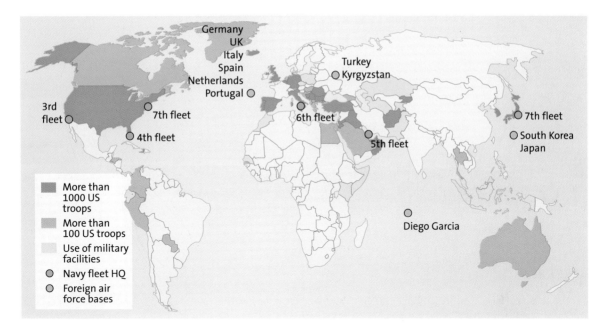

Figure 2.2
US military forces worldwide in 2008

- US forces have been stationed in Europe since 1945, initially to combat the spread of communism from the USSR. Today these forces are seen as countering the threat of a resurgent Russia.
- The US military presence in Asia also dates from 1945. After the surrender of Japan in 1945, US forces stayed on in the region because it was the eastern edge of the USSR. After the communist revolution in China in 1949 the USA applied a policy of containment, effectively encircling China and the USSR with forces in Asia and the western Pacific. Singapore, Taiwan, South Korea and the Philippines became key US allies in the fight to stop the spread of communism and the Korean and Vietnam Wars were fought for this reason.
- US forces also protect key shipping routes and what are referred to as 'choke points'. These are narrow shipping lanes through which huge volumes of oil pass (Table 2.3), which the USA depends on. The large military presence in the Middle East protects the world's most important oil fields and in recent years has grown to cope with the 'war on terror' in Iran and Afghanistan. The USA tends to give aid, in the form of economic development assistance and military aid to 'choke point' countries (Table 2.3).

Table 2.3
Shipping 'choke points'

Shipping choke point	Volume of oil passing through per day, 2006 (billions of barrels)	Controlling country/countries	Economic and military aid from the USA in 2007 (millions of dollars)
Suez Canal	4.5	Egypt	1972 to Egypt
Panama Canal	0.5	Panama	28.4 to Panama
Straits of Malacca	15	Singapore, Indonesia	7 to Singapore; 244 to Indonesia
Straits of Hormuz	17	UAE, Oman, Iran	12 to the UAE; 16 to Oman
Bab el Mandab Strait	3.3	Yemen, Djibouti, Eritrea	38 to Yemen; 13.4 to Djibouti; 3 to Eritrea
Turkish Straits	2.4	Turkey	29.8 to Turkey

Data: Energy Information Administration and USAID

Cameron Dunn

Figure 2.3
The USS Reagan
*manoeuvring in San
Diego harbour*

No country in the world has military hardware to match that of the USA. The USA has ten Nimitz class nuclear-powered super carriers (Figure 2.3), each with over 80 aircraft and an unlimited range. The USS *Reagan* was launched in 2001 at a cost of around $4.5 billion — equivalent to the GDP of Madagascar for that year. The USA has over 70 nuclear-powered submarines capable of firing Trident nuclear missiles and Cruise ballistic missiles. All of these vessels are capable of circling the globe and threatening, or attacking, almost any location on earth. The US Air Force has over 5000 aircraft including 'stealth' bombers such as the B-2, extreme fighter jets such as the F-22A Raptor, and unmanned reconnaissance aircraft like the RQ-4 Global Hawk. The USA also maintains a network of spy satellites in orbit, which effectively means it can observe the entire world — although the capabilities of these satellites are kept secret.

Trade

Table 2.1 shows that the USA and EU have broadly equal numbers of the top 500 transnational corporations (TNCs), followed by Japan and China. TNCs are important for superpower status for a number of reasons:

■ They generate enormous wealth. In 2008, the top 50 TNCs in the USA had a combined turnover of nearly $5 trillion. TNCs provide jobs, tax payments and investment that benefit the home country.

■ They invest huge sums in research and development. Notice how in Table 2.1 the number of patent filings for new technologies and inventions mirrors the number of TNCs. Successful patent filings generate wealth from royalty and licence fees; in 2005 just seven countries accounted for 70% of global royalty and licence fee revenue with the USA alone collecting $23 billion.

■ As TNCs are global, they spread their global brands around the world. Many of these are synonymous with their country of origin such as Nike, Coca-Cola, Sony

Contemporary Case Studies

and BP. In the 2008 Interbrand survey of global brand value, 52 of the top 100 most well-known global brands were from the USA.

- TNCs have complex production and trade systems which have contributed significantly to globalisation, interconnectedness and wealth creation.

Given the importance of trade in wealth creation, it is not surprising that the EU and USA both have their own trade blocs to facilitate free trade. In the EU this is the European Economic Area (EEA) or 'single market' and in the USA it is the North American Free Trade Agreement (NAFTA) between the USA, Canada and Mexico. In addition, the USA and EU have agreements that allow much free trade between the two blocs. Critics argue that free-trade blocs simply increase trade between the already wealthy and impose trade restrictions on those outside the bloc.

Trade patterns tend to reinforce the status quo. Table 2.4 shows inter- and intra-regional trade flow in manufactured goods in 2007 as a proportion of all trade in goods.

Table 2.4 shows that:

- most trade is within already wealthy regions; 53% of all trade in goods is intra-regional within Europe, Asia and North America
- trade between Asia, Europe and North America accounts for a further 23% of all trade in goods
- the remainder of world trade in goods (24%) has to be shared out among the rest of the world
- some regions with emerging and regional powers, such as Russia, the Middle East and South America, have a very small slice of the trade cake

Table 2.4
Interregional and intraregional trade in goods, 2007

Over 5% ▭ 1%–4.9% ▭ Under 1% ▭ No data = 0.1% or less		Destination						
		North America	South & Central America	Europe	Russia/ Central Asia	Africa	Middle East	Asia
Origin	North America	7.7	0.9	2.4		0.2	0.4	2.7
	South and Central America	1.1	0.9	0.7				0.5
	Europe	3.7	0.6	31.0	1.2	1.0	1.1	3.1
	Russia/Central Asia	0.2		2.1	0.7			0.4
	Africa	0.7		1.3		0.3		0.6
	Middle East	0.6		0.9		0.2	0.6	2.9
	Asia	6.0	0.6	5.1	0.4	0.6	0.9	13.9

THE UK AND ZAMBIA: DEPENDENCY THEORY

Case study 5

Zambia was once the UK colony of Northern Rhodesia. It gained its independence in 1964. By the standards of sub-Saharan Africa Zambia has had a relatively peaceful postcolonial history, not having suffered from war and internal conflict like many of its neighbours. Zambia has the major disadvantage of being landlocked but it has large areas of good farmland growing sugar and coffee — some estimates suggest only 20% of the useable land is farmed — and vast copper reserves.

Figure 2.4
*GDP per capita
UK and Zambia,
1960–2005*

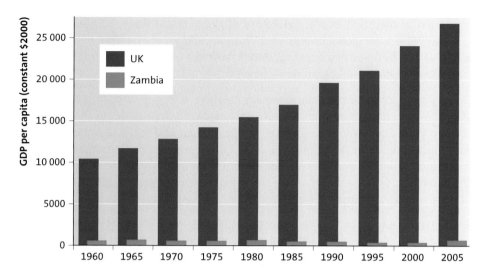

Figure 2.4 shows the startlingly different paths of GDP per capita for the UK and Zambia since 1960. Per person, Zambians were no better off in 2005 than when independence was gained in 1964, whereas in the UK income growth has been continuous. How can we explain this? It is partly to do with population growth. Zambia's economy needs to grow by 6–7% per year just to keep pace with its expanding population. However, China and India managed to grow by 8–10% during the decade 1998–2008, so why not Zambia?

In the 1960s, some left-wing academics began to argue that despite independence many developing African, Asian and Latin American nations existed in a state of **dependency** and underdevelopment. The political economist Andre Gunder Frank outlined his dependency theory in the mid 1960s. In *The Development of Underdevelopment* (1972), Frank stated that:

> ...contemporary underdevelopment is in large part the historical product of past and continuing economic and other relations between the satellite underdeveloped and the now developed metropolitan countries. Furthermore, these relations are an essential part of the capitalist system on a world scale as a whole.

Frank saw 'satellite' (periphery) countries as providing a range of services to metropolitan (core) countries:

- cheap commodities, such as oil, copper, coffee and cocoa
- labour in the form of migration, especially 'brain drain' migration of skilled workers
- markets for manufactured goods, and locations for investment such as mines and dams for hydroelectric power (HEP)

For their part, the developed countries controlled the development of developing nations by setting the prices paid for commodities, interfering in economies via the World Bank and International Monetary Fund and using economic and military aid to 'buy' the loyalty of satellite states. Dependency theorists argue that developed capitalist countries have no interest in the economic development of poor nations because such development would rob them of a cheap source of materials and labour.

This state of dependency is sometimes referred to as **neocolonialism**. The developed world uses trade and economic power to control developing countries as if they were still colonies. For Zambia this has meant:

- running up huge debts, totalling over $6 billion in 2000 and then having to follow a policy of economic liberalisation under the World Bank's Highly Indebted Poor Countries Initiative (HIPC) in order to have its debt written down. Some see the HIPC scheme as a way of developed countries controlling the developing world.
- selling copper at a price set on international markets. In 2008–09, this varied between US$8700 and US$2900 per tonne, making revenue planning very difficult.
- nationalising the copper mines in the 1970s in an attempt to take control of the industry, only to be forced to privatise them in 2001 as part of the HIPC initiative. Future investment in copper mining will rely in large part upon the willingness of foreign investors.
- that by 2006, around 50% of Zambia's skilled medical professionals had left the country, many to work in the UK

An argument against dependency theory is that some countries *have* developed since 1945. The Asian Tiger economies and other NICs and RICs have seen strong economic growth, which surely indicates that countries can break out of the dependency model.

5 — *Using case studies*

Question

(a) **Assess the role trade plays in maintaining the status of superpowers.**
(b) **Why does the USA worry about the 'choke points' in Table 2.3?**

Guidance

(a) Trade is key to generating wealth, which is a key part of superpower status. Without wealth it would be difficult for a superpower to project itself globally. Note that Table 2.4 suggests trade creates a self-supporting system where the superpowers and emerging powers largely trade with each other. Trade blocs and agreements support this.

(b) Choke points are vulnerable to terrorism, war or the controlling state deciding to shut down the trade route, or to charge excessively for its use. The USA only gave the Panama Canal Zone back to Panama in 1979. The USA worries about choke points due to its dependence on foreign oil imports which generally pass through one or more of them.

Cultural dominance

The USA today, and the British Empire in the past, have both been accused of **cultural imperialism**. This is the process whereby a major power imposes its cultural ideas and values on less-powerful peoples or nations. During the age of empire the UK attempted to impose Christianity, cricket, English law and the English language on its colonies. Some aspects of culture, like cricket, were accepted while others were resisted. In the postcolonial era, cultural imperialism is a more subtle process because superpowers do not rule colonies directly. The USA is accused of cultural imperialism through processes such as:

- the spread of English as the international language of business, particularly by TNCs
- the global dominance of US media companies such as Disney Corp and Time–Warner

- the spread of US electronic technology such as Microsoft Windows, Google search and Apple media players
- the spread of the culture of western consumerism, especially into Asia, led by global brands may of which are based in the USA

It is difficult to identify exactly what the 'Western values' which the USA is accused of spreading are but they might be summarised as:

- **Democracy** — the belief that a developed society is one where everyone has the right to vote
- **Individualism** — the belief that individuals should have the right to pursue their own actions and dreams
- **Consumerism** — the belief that wealth, and the ability to buy goods and services, leads to happiness
- **Technology** — the belief that problems can be solved by using technology, especially high-end technology
- **Economic freedom** — the belief that markets should be free, and people should be at liberty to make money how they choose

There is no doubt that these values do jar with the values of other cultures and nations. For instance, there is no universal acceptance that Western democracy is the best political system. Some cultures might value community and collectivism over individualism. Cultural imperialism is accused of undermining other cultures, their values and traditions. It is certainly the case that as societies become ever more tied into the global system of trade and exchange they do change and have adopted 'Western' patterns of work, family and consumption. Is this a positive or negative development? To a large extent the answer to this question is a matter of opinion.

Case study 6 — MCDONALD'S: GLOBAL SUPERPOWER?

In 1993, the American sociologist George Ritzer wrote a book entitled *The McDonaldization of Society*. Ritzer's central argument was that fast-food-style systems would eventually take over the world because McDonald's, and other fast-food outlets such as Starbucks, had hit upon a universal recipe for making money that could be applied the world over:

- **Reducing costs** — in McDonald's, customers act as unpaid workers; queuing up for food (no waiters), placing rubbish in the bins provided, getting their own straws and ketchup. This maximises profit. In the USA, customers fill their own drinks.
- **Quantity** — focusing on size rather than quality, e.g. using terms such as 'Big Mac', 'Whopper' and 'go large', so that consumers perceive value for money to be more important than quality.
- **Predictability** — the idea that 'sameness' sells because people feel more comfortable with what they know. This might explain why Hollywood produces endless movie sequels.
- **Replacing humans** — mechanising the production process using factory farming, automatic ovens, coffee makers etc. because humans are more expensive and less reliable.

McDonald's, Starbucks and others have applied this 'recipe' the world over with astounding success and globalised Western consumption (Figures 2.5 and 2.6; Table 2.5).

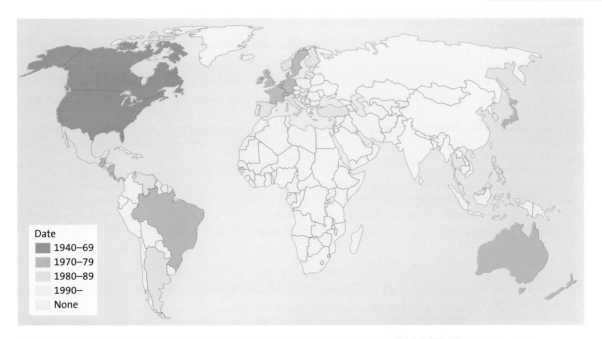

Figure 2.5
Global spread of McDonald's since 1940

Date
- 1940–69
- 1970–79
- 1980–89
- 1990–
- None

McDonald's

Figure 2.6
McDonald's in Shanghai

Table 2.5
McFacts

Revenue in 2008: $23.5 billion	Sales growth by region	USA	Europe	Asia/ Middle East/Africa	Other countries
Customers served per day in 2008: 58 million	2008	4.0%	8.5%	9.0%	13.0%
Number of restaurants in 2008: 32 000 in 109 countries/territories	2007	4.5%	7.6%	10 .6%	10.8%
	2006	5.2%	5.8%	5.5%	9.4%

Table 2.6 McDonald's: good corporation, bad corporation?

Transnational monster?	Corporate responsibility?
Jobs are often referred to as 'dead-end' McJobs	Jobs for around 1.5 million people, often in areas with few jobs
Leakage of revenue out of host countries back to USA	Significant tax revenue for the USA from global profits
Suburban and drive-through restaurants encourage car use	Provides people with low-cost, accessible food that is of reasonable quality
Free toys given with happy meals, encourages an 'I want that' culture of consumerism	Many restaurants have playgrounds encouraging kids to exercise
Food is bland and dull, and undermines local and traditional foods	Products are adapted to local tastes, and ingredients are locally sourced
Ingredients are low quality and bad for the environment, e.g. encouraging deforestation for cattle ranching	Fair trade coffee has been introduced, and milk used in UK restaurants is organic — meat is halal in regions where this is required
Food is basically high fat and encourages an unhealthy diet and obesity	Healthy options have been introduced, such as the Australian Lean Beef Burger and nutritional information is available with each meal

This is not to say that McDonald's food is identical the world over; it has required adaptation, or **glocalisation**, to local markets but the process of making and serving the food follows the same basic recipe for success.

- In New Zealand, McDonald's offers a 'Kiwi Big Breakfast' and a burger called 'The Boss'.
- In India, much of the menu is vegetarian, or based on chicken such as the 'Chicken Maharaja Mac'.
- In the Middle East, the 'McArabia Kofta' is wrapped in pitta bread and all meat is halal.

There is no doubt that companies such as McDonald's are global and that they have spread an American concept of consumption. Often fast-food companies spread more than just their own company brand. McDonald's contributes to the spread of Coca-Cola, and happy-meal tie-ups spread Disney characters and American movies. However, there are arguments both for and against powerful Western corporations such as McDonald's (Table 2.6).

World systems theory

A weakness with dependency theory is that it is static — the theory suggests that countries are stuck in a permanently underdeveloped state. The rise of the NIC and RIC countries since 1980 suggests the world is more complex than a simple super-power core and undeveloped periphery. Immanuel Wallerstein developed world systems theory in the 1970s (see Figure 2.7). This theory argues that the world is divided into:

- core regions — the OECD countries and the USA and EU superpowers
- semi-periphery regions — the NICs and RICs of Latin America and Asia, including the emerging powers such as India and China
- periphery regions — the rest of the developing world

Wallerstein's theory has the flexibility to recognise that countries may change regional group over time. In the future, some areas such as China may move into the core world. A more classically Marxist theory such as Frank's dependency theory

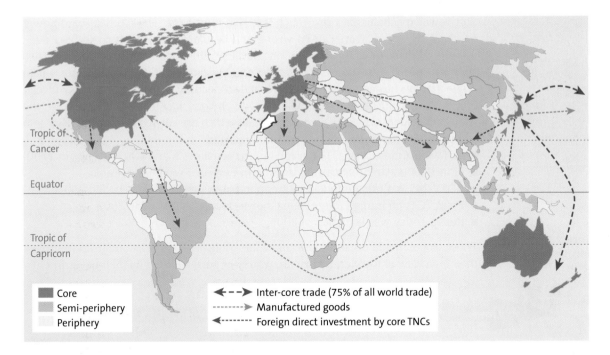

Core
Semi-periphery
Periphery

◄--► Inter-core trade (75% of all world trade)
------► Manufactured goods
◄------- Foreign direct investment by core TNCs

is more rigid, simply seeing the world as divided into 'owners' (rich countries) and 'workers' (poor countries). In the world systems theory model:

■ Core countries use semi-periphery countries as cheap locations to make manufactured goods, such as the Free Trade Zones of China, or as locations for cheap services such as the call centres of Bangalore. Core countries get large returns on the foreign investment they make in semi-periphery countries.

■ Periphery regions provide raw materials to supply manufacturing industry in semi-periphery and consumption in core regions. The periphery is furthest down the supply chain and therefore least able to benefit from profits made by selling finished goods and services.

World systems theory seems to fit today's world reasonably well, whereas dependency theory fits a 'north–south' world which existed up until the mid 1980s. A valid criticism of world systems theory is that it is really a description of the world's patterns of power and wealth rather than an explanation of them.

Figure 2.7
World systems
theory geography

Hard power versus soft power

A useful way of examining how superpowers maintain their influence is to examine 'hard' versus 'soft' mechanisms of power. This theory was developed by the political economist Joseph Nye. Hard power is the military might that superpowers possess. It is overt, 'in your face' power. Soft power is more subtle and covert. It is used to gradually persuade people that the superpowers' view is the right one. In some ways soft power supports Gramsci's theory of hegemony. Soft power brings us around to the superpowers' way of thinking without us even realising. Table 2.7 shows the spectrum of power mechanisms.

Soft-power mechanisms carry much less risk than hard. The ultimate hard-power mechanism is war. Wars can go wrong and be ultimately lost. It could be argued that the US invasion of Iraq went wrong because although it overthrew Saddam Hussein it alienated much of the Middle East and Muslim world. Some politicians would argue that this has contributed to decreased US security, e.g. the global terror threat. Soft power has increased in popularity. One obvious way this can be seen is in the use of state-sponsored global news channels which are carried on satellite television alongside Sky News, the BBC, CNN and Fox News:

- CCTV-9 is China Central Television international news and was launched in 2000.
- France 24 began broadcasting in 2006 in English, French and Arabic.
- NDTV-247 is a private Indian international news channel launched in 2003.
- Press TC is an Iranian international news channel launched in 2007.
- Russia Today was launched in 2005.

Table 2.7
Mechanisms of power

These global media organisations allow the countries they originate from to project their own view of the world. Most are wholly or partly funded by their governments.

Hard power ←	→ Soft power	
Military presence and force	**Aid and trade**	**Culture and ideology**
Large air, naval and land forces	Favouring certain trade partners by reducing import tariffs	Using the media to promote a particular image and message
Nuclear weapons	Trade blocs and alliances	Exporting culture in the form of film and television, or globally recognised brands
Military bases in foreign countries giving geographical reach	Providing allies with economic and technical assistance	
Military alliances such as NATO	Using aid to influence policy or keep allies happy	Gradually persuading doubters that a particular action or view is in their interests
Diplomatic threats to use force if negotiation fails, and the use of force	Using economic sanctions against countries	

6 Question

(a) Should TNCs such as McDonald's be considered as superpowers in their own right?

(b) In the early twenty-first century, which is more important, hard or soft power?

Guidance

(a) Large TNCs are certainly powerful. Many have global workforces equivalent to large cities and annual sales that dwarf the economies of smaller developing countries. TNCs can influence government and are a force for development. Culturally, it could be argued that they have as much influence as governments. Powerful as they are, TNCs lack the military and political facets of a superpower country.

(b) Soft power is considered a key tool in the ammunition belt of a modern superpower or emerging power. We all stared in awe at the Beijing Olympics, and as far as the Chinese were concerned we were 'on message'. Recent conflicts, such as the invasion of Iraq and the engagement in Afghanistan, show the limitations of hard power. Controlling events on the ground, as well as the media's portrayal of conflict, is virtually impossible.

Using case studies

Superpowers and conflict

The nature of conflict

Conflict occurs when two or more parties disagree (Table 3.1). In some circumstances conflict can escalate into a military clash between parties — in other words a war. Conflicting parties can range in scale from individuals in an argument up to a global conflict such as the Second World War, when the world essentially divided into the Allies, the Axis and neutral countries. Conflict is caused in a number of ways, with some conflicts being significantly easier to 'solve' than others. In many cases conflicts have multiple causes and these can be difficult to unravel in order to find the original cause.

Conflict need not lead to warfare and usually does not. War is prevented by:

- **diplomacy** — conflicting parties are encouraged to settle their differences through discussion. Often a third country or international organisation, such as the United Nations, acts as a peace broker.
- **negotiation** — this may involve making a deal, or offering some form of compensation or trade-off to solve a dispute.
- **isolation** — countries may be isolated politically and economically by the use of sanctions or by withdrawing trade or communication links.

In some cases war is averted because both parties recognise that the stakes are too high, i.e. the benefits of war would not outweigh the costs. This is the case with the long-running territorial dispute between China, India, Japan and Russia.

Table 3.1
Causes of conflict

Justice and rights	Some conflicts are seen as being 'just' because they attempt to right a wrong — for example freeing an enslaved or conquered people. Wars of independence are often fought on the basis that they are just wars to give people the right of self-determination.
Morals and values	Conflicting cultural views and norms are often reinforced by different religions. Different groups have differences over what is 'wrong' and 'right'. Muslims view women's veils as 'right' whereas many Westerners view veils as 'wrong'. This type of conflict includes different political ideologies such as capitalism versus communism.
Resources	Conflict can occur due to the need for water, land or mineral resources. This may mean someone else's territory must be taken to obtain these.
Ethnicity	Many conflicts are based on ethnic and racial differences (often mixed with religious/value differences) and the desire of one group to dominate a territory by expelling another group.

Outright war between emerging powers over relatively minor territorial disputes is unlikely; instead they are 'shelved' sometimes for decades. From a geopolitical perspective it is possible to identify a hierarchy of conflicts:

- **Internal conflict** means a civil war or coup d'état in which the only parties are those within a country and there is minimal outside influence. The 1983–2009 war between the government and the Tamil Tigers in Sri Lanka has been largely internal, with a brief period of Indian involvement 1987–90.
- **Proxy conflict** occurs when outside influences are involved in what appears to be an internal conflict, perhaps by supplying arms, finance or other assistance. The Angolan civil war 1975–2002 is a good example. Immediately following independence from Portugal in 1975, war broke out between the communist Popular Movement for the Liberation of Angola (MPLA), supported by the USSR, and the National Liberation Front of Angola (FNLA), supported by the USA, China and Zaire. The National Union for the Total Liberation of Angola (UNITA) was a third warring faction, supported by the USA and South Africa.
- **External conflict** occurs when two or more nation states are directly at war with each other but the conflict is confined to one region. Most international support for the three factions in Angola was indirect (e.g. military equipment, training and intelligence) but Cuba and South Africa deployed troops in Angola.
- **Global conflict** occurs when numerous countries take sides creating different theatres of war in widely spread regions. The Second World War is an example; fighting occurred in Europe, Africa and Asia and the superpowers of the day were directly involved.

Superpower conflict

The American social scientist A. F. K. Organski developed the power transition theory in the late 1950s. He argued that power approximates to a hierarchy of different types of state:

- superpowers — globally dominant (the hegemonic power)
- emerging powers (or 'great powers') — rivals to the superpowers
- regional (or 'middle') powers — not powerful enough to challenge those above them
- small powers — the remaining, weak nations

Organski argued that the superpowers organise global systems in their own interests. This might be seen in the way that the USA organised the United Nations, IMF, World Trade Organization and G8 in the postwar period, in order to promote the idea of global capitalism. Organski also suggested that superpowers have a life span of 60–90 years. During this time emerging powers 'catch up' and eventually attempt to challenge the superpower. Organski's world is one of periods of calm punctuated by periods of conflict, for example:

- The hegemony of the Netherlands was ended by the Dutch War 1672–78, allowing Britain to become the dominant power.
- Napoleon unsuccessfully challenged the hegemony of Britain during the Napoleonic wars 1803–14.

- The dominance of the British Empire was challenged by Germany and the Axis powers during the First and Second World Wars. The interwar period was a 'power vacuum' with no dominant superpower.
- After the Second World War, the USA and USSR emerged as the dominant superpowers.

It is interesting to speculate that we may now be approaching a period of conflict as China, India and others are increasingly challenging the postwar consensus of a world dominated by the USA. It may be the case that the challenge will take an economic and political form, as an all-out global conflict in a nuclear age is in no one's interest. Alternatively, the conflict may take the form of a series of proxy wars. These wars occur when superpowers and emerging powers fight for dominance in a third country, such as the Angolan conflict. This allows dominance to be determined without resorting to full-scale regional or global conflict.

MEDDLING IN SUDAN

Case study 7

Sudan gained its independence from Britain on 1 January 1956. However, in the previous year civil war had broken out between the north and south of the country. Civil war raged from 1955–72, then again from 1983–2005. In 2003, war broke out in the western Darfur province (Figure 3.1) and has continued ever since. Sudan has enjoyed only 11 years of peace since 1956. The conflicts since 1955 are outlined in Table 3.2.

The 2005 peace deal, signed in Nairobi, was only an interim solution. This is because it called for 6 years of peace followed by a referendum in southern Sudan in 2011. In the interim period, oil revenues are to be shared between the north and south. If the south votes for independence in 2011, will the north agree? The north could lose most of its access to oil, water and fertile farmland.

Like many African countries, Sudan's instability can be traced back, at least in part, to the legacy of colonial rule. During the first and second civil wars both Cold War superpowers supplied arms to Sudan, supporting various warring factions and corrupt governments in what amounted to a proxy war to bring Sudan into the sphere of influence of the USA or USSR. The USA switched sides in the Sudanese conflict,

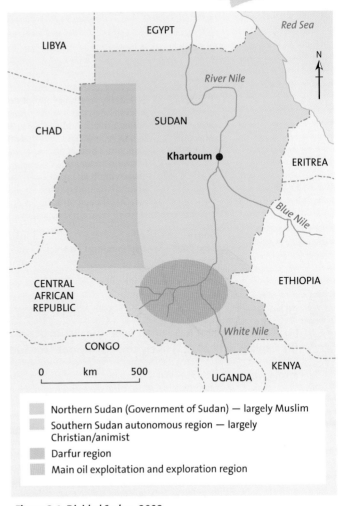

Figure 3.1 Divided Sudan, 2008

Legend:
- Northern Sudan (Government of Sudan) — largely Muslim
- Southern Sudan autonomous region — largely Christian/animist
- Darfur region
- Main oil exploitation and exploration region

supporting the north until it began to support Islamic extremists. The increasing involvement of China in Sudan and Chad has further complicated a tense situation. China is accused of supporting the Sudanese government's conflict in Darfur simply because Sudan has oil which China needs.

Table 3.2
Chronology of war in Sudan

Conflict	Cause	Impacts	Superpower involvement
First Sudanese civil war, 1955–72	Southern Sudan (see Figure 3.1) demands independence from northern Sudan	500 000 deaths	During the colonial era Britain had separated the north and south, even banning indigenous travel between the areas. This helped promote Christianity in the animist south. It fuelled demands for two states in the postcolonial era In the 1960s, Israel, then the USSR began to supply southern Sudan with arms
Second Sudanese civil war, 1983–2005	A continuation of demands for southern independence; the north did not want to lose the south's fertile farmland and oil	2 million deaths 4 million refugees	The USA began to sell arms to the northern Sudanese government in the 1970s (up to $2 billion worth). In the early 1990s, the terrorist group Al Qaeda moved to Sudan and the USA began to isolate Sudan, especially after the northern government supported Saddam Hussein in the First Gulf War In 2001, with Al Qaeda expelled from Sudan, the USA began to act as peace-broker, leading to the 2005 ceasefire
Darfur conflict, 2003 onwards	Essentially an ethnic war between the nomadic black-Arab Janjaweed militias (supported by the northern Sudanese government) and non-Arab tribal farmers (the Fur, Masalit and others)	Estimates range up to 300 000 deaths 2.5 million refugees	Arms have been supplied to the Sudanese government by China and Russia and PetroChina invested $15 billion in Sudanese oil fields In 2009, the International Criminal Court in the Hague issued an arrest warrant for Sudanese President Omar al-Bashir on charges of genocide
Chad–Sudan war, 2005 onwards	The conflict in Darfur spills over into neighbouring Chad	Estimates suggest 300 000 refugees	Despite a peace treaty brokered by Libya in 2006, the conflict has continued. Chad has received arms from the USA and China is beginning to show interest in Chad

7

Using case studies

Question

(a) **To what extent has Sudan been the victim of proxy warfare?**

(b) **Explain why 2011 is likely to be a key date for Sudan.**

Guidance

(a) There is strong evidence for superpower meddling in Sudan. It could be argued that the British left the country ungovernable. During the Cold War the USA, USSR and China were involved at various times, usually supporting opposite factions in the perennial north-versus-south conflict. The side-switching engaged by the superpowers created a highly unstable situation.

(b) Sudan's 2005–11 'peace' is really a stop-gap measure which ended the north–south conflict by putting its final resolution on hold until 2011. There is a real danger of a split in the future, and a resumption of war. The south contains the main oil fields.

GLOBAL TERRORISM

8:46 a.m. on 11 September 2001 can be identified as the time the 'war on terror' began. This was the moment that American Airlines Flight 11 was flown into the north tower of the Word Trade Center in New York. This was not the first terrorist attack on the USA, or other Western democracies, but it was the most iconic. Modern usage of the phrase 'war on terror' began on 20 September 2001 when President George W. Bush uttered the words: 'Our war on terror begins with al Qaeda.'

Bush was referring to the extreme Islamist organisation led by Osama Bin Laden. Al Qaeda's conflict with the USA dates to the first Gulf War in 1990. Al Qaeda objected to the USA's military operations in Kuwait, Saudi Arabia and, eventually, Iraq. Bin Laden, a citizen of Saudi Arabia, was expelled from that country to Sudan for speaking out against the Saudi government. Today, he is thought to be in Afghanistan or northern Pakistan. Since 1990, Al Qaeda has launched numerous attacks on the 'West' (Figure 3.2) in a dispersed global conflict which pits Western, largely Christian, capitalist democracies against Middle eastern Islamic theocracies and monarchies. Of course, the overwhelming majority of Muslims are not Islamic fundamentalists wishing to overthrow the USA. However, there are significant tensions between the West and the Muslim world:

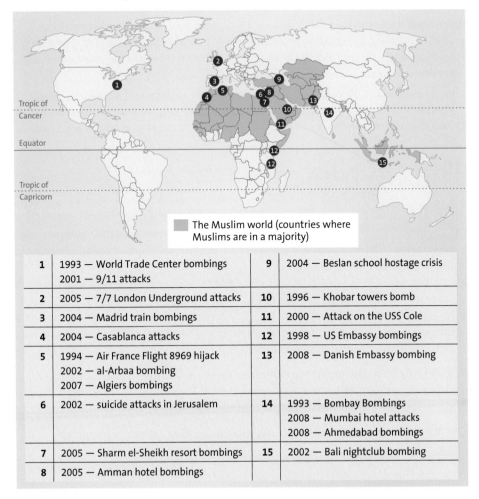

Figure 3.2
Global terrorism since 1993

The Muslim world (countries where Muslims are in a majority)

1	1993 — World Trade Center bombings 2001 — 9/11 attacks	9	2004 — Beslan school hostage crisis
2	2005 — 7/7 London Underground attacks	10	1996 — Khobar towers bomb
3	2004 — Madrid train bombings	11	2000 — Attack on the USS Cole
4	2004 — Casablanca attacks	12	1998 — US Embassy bombings
5	1994 — Air France Flight 8969 hijack 2002 — al-Arbaa bombing 2007 — Algiers bombings	13	2008 — Danish Embassy bombing
6	2002 — suicide attacks in Jerusalem	14	1993 — Bombay Bombings 2008 — Mumbai hotel attacks 2008 — Ahmedabad bombings
7	2005 — Sharm el-Sheikh resort bombings	15	2002 — Bali nightclub bombing
8	2005 — Amman hotel bombings		

- The West, particularly the USA, is seen as acting in its own interests with little or no regard for the sovereignty of Muslim countries. The first Gulf War, the invasion of Iraq in 2003 and Afghanistan in 2001 and even the Soviet invasion of Afghanistan in 1979 are all seen as examples of such interference.
- There is a perceived imposition of Western democracy on countries such as Iraq, a political system which has never been part of the Islamic world.
- The Western powers have been unable to find a solution to the Israel–Palestine conflict and there is perceived USA bias towards Israel's position.
- There is long-term economic stagnation in many Arab countries, combined with an over-reliance on oil exports. Male youth unemployment in North Africa and the Middle East is typically over 20%, which some argue makes the region a breeding ground for extremism.

On a more ideological level, Muslim extremism could be seen as a reaction to America's unchallenged global hegemony. It is possible to view the USA as an imperial power and imperial powers attract attacks against them. Perhaps it is no surprise that global terrorism is a product of the post-Cold War, unipolar world.

The future of global terrorism, sponsored by Islamic extremists is not at all certain. For the terror threat to subside it is likely that the West will need to withdraw from its direct involvement in Iraq and Afghanistan. A peace deal between Israel and Palestine, probably involving the creation of a Palestinian State may also be needed. The new US President Barack Obama did signal a significant shift in USA–Islamic relations in June 2009 when he said:

> I have come here to seek a new beginning between the United States and Muslims around the world, one based upon mutual interest and mutual respect. America and Islam are not exclusive, and need not be in competition.   (4 June 2009, Cairo, Egypt)

The Olympics

An interesting way of examining the changing status of superpowers is to explore the Olympic Games. The summer Olympiad is a global event and the Olympics have become an important global stage and brand. Simply staging the Olympics seems to confer a particular status on the host:
- In 1998, Seoul in South Korea used the Olympics to confirm its status as the most successful of the first generation NICs.
- In 2008, the Beijing Olympics in China was designed to launch that country onto the world stage (Figure 3.3). The 2010 Shanghai Expo will ensure that China remains in the international spotlight.

In 1980, the USA boycotted the Moscow Olympics because of the Soviet invasion of Afghanistan. In 1984, the USSR and Warsaw Pact countries boycotted the Los Angeles Olympics largely as 'revenge' for the 1980 boycott.

The Olympic medals table also reveals something about superpower status (Table 3.3).

TopFoto

The 1952 games were the first Cold War Olympics, with the USA out in front as the country that recovered most quickly from the Second World War. Over the next few decades the communist USSR and Warsaw Pact countries gradually overtook the USA — they saw the Olympics as a chance to 'shine' on the world stage. We now know that, particularly in East Germany, performance enhancing drugs were used regularly. The 1996 games were the first true post-Cold War games, with the USA back on top. In the last two decades, the emerging power of China has gradually caught the USA, leading to the Chinese team's triumph in Beijing. The space race represents another window into superpower status.

Figure 3.3
The Beijing Olympic Games opening ceremony at the Bird's Nest Stadium

Olympics	Most gold medals	Second place	Third place
1952, Helsinki	USA, 40	USSR, 21	Hungary, 16
1972, Munich	USSR, 50	USA, 33	East Germany, 20
1988, Seoul	USSR, 55	East Germany, 37	USA, 36
1996, Atlanta	USA, 44	Russia, 26	Germany, 20
2000, Sydney	USA, 36	Russia, 32	China, 28
2008, Beijing	China, 51	USA, 36	Russia, 23

Table 3.3
The gold medal tally for six summer Olympics

The conquest of space has been a dream of humans for centuries, but it was only in the Cold War era that getting into space became a possibility. This was because Nazi Germany had developed complex rocket technology during the Second World War (the V1 and V2 rockets developed by Dr Werner von Braun), which subsequently fell into the hands of the USA and USSR.

In 1957, the American public was stunned to learn that the communist USSR had launched a satellite, Sputnik 1, into orbit around the Earth. Sputnik 2 followed 1 month later carrying Laika, the first animal in space (Laika was never intended to return to Earth, so was space's first casualty). In 1961, Yuri Gagarin became the world's first astronaut — his Vostok orbiter circled the Earth. The USA managed the same feat in 1962. The two superpowers then embarked on a race to the Moon that stretched the financial, human and technical resources of the two nations to the limit:

- Vostok 6 took the first woman into space in 1963
- Voskhod 1 carried the first two-person mission in 1964
- Voskhod 2 conducted the first space walk in 1965

Khrushchev, the Soviet leader, was less keen on a manned Moon mission than President Kennedy (and President Johnson after Kennedy's assassination in 1963) because of the huge financial cost. After 1966, the USA began to pull ahead in the space race culminating in the Apollo 11 Moon landing in 1969. After this the USA dominated, especially following the 1981 launch of the Space Shuttle, Columbia. Why did the superpowers engage in the space race?

- Prestige was a key reason; any space 'first' by either side was as good as saying 'capitalism is better than communism' or vice versa.
- Technology took giant leaps forward, especially in the field of electronic communication, computers, materials science and rocketry. This last technology was closely linked to nuclear missile delivery.

Figure 3.4
Twenty-first-century space race

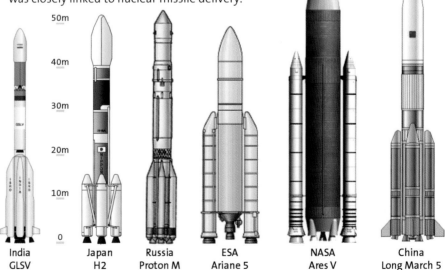

| India GLSV | Japan H2 | Russia Proton M | ESA Ariane 5 | NASA Ares V | China Long March 5 |

- Eventually, pure science experiments were conducted in space, in the weightless environment.
- Closely linked to the space race were developments in communication and spy satellites that continue to meet defence and economic needs.

Today, there is a renewed space race, but it is no longer a two-horse race, as Figure 3.4 shows. In an increasingly multipolar world is it not surprising that numerous nations are engaged in space research and development. The current aims of the various national space programmes are very different:

- The Indian Space Research Organisation is focused on developing a heavy-lift version of its GLSV rocket to make India self-sufficient in satellite launching.
- The Japan Aerospace Exploration Agency is focused on unmanned missions, satellite technology and research, as is the European Space Agency.
- Russia continues to plan manned space flight and has sophisticated technology that is not matched by funding.
- China launched its first manned space flight in 2003 as part of the Shenzhou programme. China plans a space station and a manned Moon mission by 2020. This is likely to bring China and the USA into direct competition, as NASA plans to return to the Moon to build a Moon base by 2020, as a first step to reaching Mars by 2037.

8 Using case studies

Question

(a) **Explain why the Olympic Games and space race were such potent symbols of the Cold War era.**

(b) **What does the twenty-first-century space race tell us about the emerging powers?**

Guidance

(a) Both the Olympic Games and space race were proxies for all-out warfare. They allowed the East and West to compete for dominance on the world stage with nothing to lose put pride. Technology and sporting prowess were on show for all the world to see and the winners were effectively claiming their ideology to be the best.

(b) Use the space race information, and Figure 3.4, to judge which of the BRICs seems to be closest to the USA in terms of space technology.

Forget North–South and East–West?

In 2003, an American geostrategist called Thomas Barnett published a new geo-political map of the world (Figure 3.5). Barnett's map looks very different to the East versus West Cold War map shown in Figure 1.5 and to a standard North versus South development gap map. Barnett, politically close to George W. Bush and therefore right-wing, identifies three types of country:

- **Core countries** are those that are integrated into the world economy. These are the connected nations in terms of trade flows, TNC operations and the use of the internet and other communications. These countries have a big economic stake in the globalised economy and play a role in international organisations and decision making. The core includes the superpowers and some emerging powers.

- **Gap countries** are those that are poorly connected and poorly integrated into the capitalist world economy. Most are poor and some are so-called failed states such as North Korea and Somalia. They are often the location of conflict and many need humanitarian aid.
- **Seam countries** are those that are close to the gap countries and often form a 'buffer zone' between the core and the gap. Some are emerging powers and all have a regional power base. They tend to lie just within, or just outside, what Barnett called the boundary of the non-integrating gap.

Barnett's argument is that countries such as the USA need to support the seam states because they play an important role in maintaining regional peace.

This type of analysis of global geopolitics in the early part of the twenty-first century is open to question on a number of grounds:

- First, core and seam countries are essentially those that are similar to the USA and share 'Western' values to some extent. Gap nations are seen as being dangerous and anti-American (or at least not pro-American). This means the map is very much a US view of its friends and foes.
- Second, some regions, such as the oil-rich states of the Middle East (U.A.E., Qatar), are increasingly integrated into the global economy but are identified as part of the gap. The map could almost be seen as arguing that all Muslim countries are part of the problem.

Figure 3.5
Core, gap and seam analysis

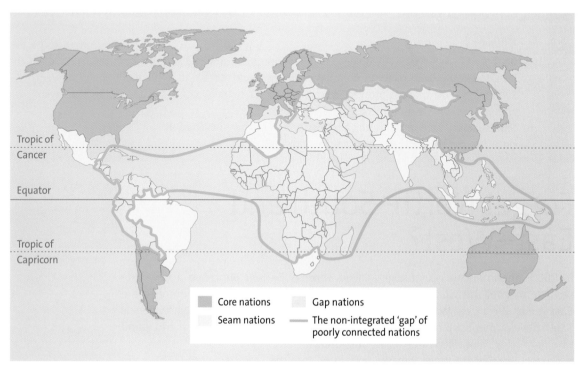

- Third, the most globalised countries are part of the core, which implies that more globalisation is the solution for an insecure world. Apart from seeming simplistic, critics would point to the often unfair nature of globalised trade and sweatshop-style factories and question whether globalisation is good.

Barnett's ideas are similar in many ways to the ideas of Wallerstein, and the 'father' of geopolitics, Sir Halford MacKinder. Both these men divided the world up into vast geographical regions to which they assigned strategic importance. Wallerstein's world systems theory uses essentially economic regions (core, semi-periphery and periphery); Barnett's tripartite division is more based on political stability and values. MacKinder was an Edwardian geographer who, in 1904, published his heartland theory in an article entitled 'The geographical pivot of history' in the *Geographical Journal*. MacKinder considered that Central Asia (now incorporating Iran, the Caucasus, Kazakhstan and much of Russia) was the pivotal geographical area of the world — whichever superpower controlled this resource-rich region could control the rest of the world. Even today, over 100 years after his theory was published, the region is a troubled and important one as it lies at the boundary between Asia, the Muslim world and Europe.

Emerging powers

Emerging powers

It is not possible to know what the geopolitical landscape will be like in 20, 30 or 50 years' time, but is seems fairly certain that it will differ from today's. A commonly held view is that the world will be more fragmented — a multipolar world, rather than a unipolar one dominated by the USA (or the bipolar world of the Cold War).

A multipolar world suggests a world where either power is regional, or global super-powers are in more or less continuous conflict. There surely is not space for more than two true superpowers? Figure 4.1 provides an illustration of these contrasting geopolitical worlds. In Figure 4.1 the picture does change slightly, depending on how the EU is treated i.e. as a bloc, or as separate nations (as shown). In the diagram, the circles are proportional to total GDP.

Figure 4.1
Comparing geopolitical patterns

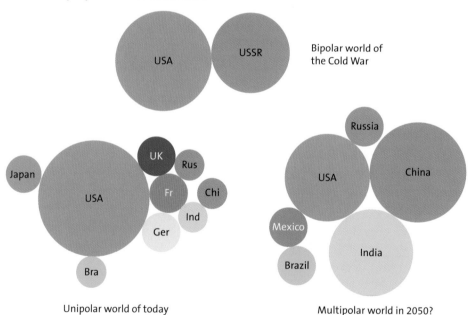

Bipolar world of the Cold War

Unipolar world of today

Multipolar world in 2050?

Much of the work on the emerging powers has been carried out by the investment bank Goldman Sachs which is based in the USA. In the 2001 report *Dreaming with BRICs — the path to 2050*, the term BRICs was first used. The BRICs are the emerging powers of Brazil, Russia, India and China. Today, these countries are still relatively small in terms of economic power (although not demographically) as is shown by Figure 4.2. At the moment, their emerging power status is based on:

Contemporary Case Studies

- vast oil reserves in Russia, estimated at around 60 billion barrels in 2007 plus the world's largest reserves of natural gas
- China's manufacturing strength and its position as 'the workshop to the world'; China is also a huge consumer market as its population exceeds 1 billion people
- India having a huge potential consumer market but a relatively small middle class; it is well known as a centre for high-tech investment
- Brazil has the most mature economy of the BRICs and a high GDP per capita of around $7000 in 2008.

In 2007, Goldman Sachs predicted that the economies of the BRICs would grow dramatically by 2050. This can be seen in Figure 4.2 — by 2050, China's economy is predicted to be by far the largest, with India and the USA broadly equal, followed by Mexico, Brazil and Russia. Because of different population sizes, per capita GDP would follow a different pattern. The USA's per capita GDP would double to around $90 000 but those of China, Mexico, Brazil and Russia would grow to lie within the $50–60 000 range (higher than per capita GDP in the USA in 2008). Only India would lag behind at around $20 000 per person, similar to the GDP of South Korea today.

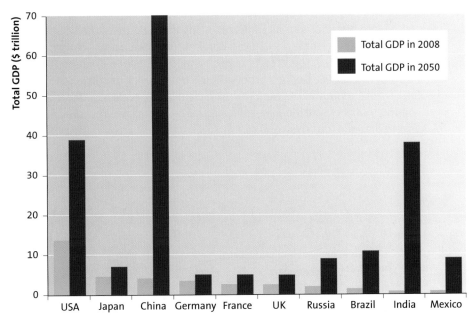

Figure 4.2
Total GDP in 2008 and projected to 2050

How likely is this scenario? Goldman Sachs' analysis has been criticised:
- The BRIC analysis dates from before the 2007–09 global financial crisis and recession. It is not fully clear how this might affect the BRICs. Russia for instance depends heavily on the oil and gas price for its wealth.
- It is unclear whether the world has enough natural resources to provide billions of people with the levels of income the Goldman Sachs analysis suggests.
- The grouping together of the four BRIC countries suggests that they are similar, but in many ways they are not. At the moment, China stands out as being significantly more powerful than the other three countries.

Stable BRICs?

Another aspect of BRICs which is troubling is their potential for instability. The current superpowers, the USA and EU, are located in stable regions. Since the Second World War, neither region has experienced significant instability:

- The 1959 Cuban revolution and subsequent Cuban missile crisis in 1962 increased tension in North America but the situation did not escalate.
- The collapse of the Berlin Wall in 1990 could have destabilised Europe, but the EU acted quickly to draw former Warsaw Pact nations into the union.
- The collapse, and subsequent fragmentation of Yugoslavia, beginning in 1990, posed a serious threat to Europe, but UN- and NATO-led peacekeeping forces acted to contain and eventually suppress the threat.

These international incidents are minor compared with the troubled nature of Asia. China, India and Russia all operate in overlapping spheres of influence and all three are nuclear powers. Within Asia, there are a large number of potential flashpoints that could easily destabilise the region and divert attention from the business of economic growth (Figure 4.3):

(1) Transcaucasia is where European Russia meets the Muslim world. This region fragmented into numerous small states following the collapse of the USSR. Many states, for example Azerbaijan, Nagorno-Karabakh, Armenia and Georgia, fought for their independence. The area is one of important mineral wealth, but disputed territory. In 2008, Georgia erupted into conflict over the disputed regions of South Ossetia and Abhkazia both of which claim independence. Georgia, however, claims that they are Georgian but occupied by Russia. The USA, EU and NATO were dragged into this conflict.

Figure 4.3
Asian flashpoints

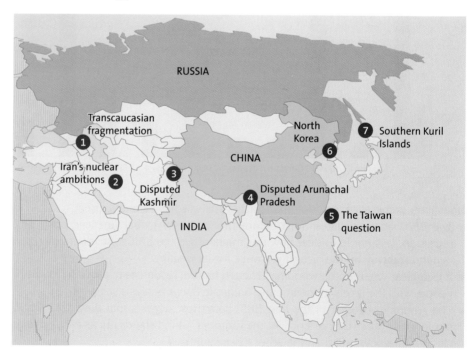

Contemporary Case Studies

(2) While bordering none of the Asian BRICs, Iran is nonetheless important. Its nuclear power and possible nuclear weapons programmes have been supported by both Russia and China. The UK, USA and Israel are strongly opposed to a nuclear Iran.

(3) Kashmir is a disputed region lying within India and Pakistan. It has been a source of continual tension and open conflict since the 1940s. India and Pakistan both have nuclear weapons and relations between the countries tend to see-saw between reasonably friendly and downright hostile. Pakistan has been destabilised since 2000 by the war in Afghanistan and by the Taliban (Muslim extremists) in its northern tribal areas.

(4) China and India have an unresolved territorial dispute in Arunachal Pradesh, which led to a brief war in 1962 and a border skirmish in 1987. India also claims that China is occupying Indian territory in Kashmir. Tibet is a further possible source of tension as the exiled Tibetan leader, the Dalai Lama, leads his government while in exile in India.

(5) Taiwan is claimed by the Chinese to be part of the People's Republic of China, but in fact Taiwan has operated as a separate country since the Chinese communist revolution in 1949. The defeated Chinese nationalists fled to Taiwan in that year. Taiwan is not recognised internationally as a country, but should China try to reclaim the territory other countries could easily become involved.

(6) North Korea is the archetypal failed state — an insular country led by a succession of ruthless dictators. North Korea has nuclear ambitions and its shaky relationships with South Korea, China, Russia and the USA could destabilise the entire region.

(7) Japan and Russia remain in a long-running dispute over the sovereignty of the small chain of islands that stretches between Hokkaido (Japan) and Kamchatka (Russia). The dispute has made no progress since the 1950s.

The conflict zones shown in Figure 4.3 trace a region sometimes referred to as the 'arc of instability'. This is a region of often unstable governments and potential flashpoints which stretches from the western Pacific, through most of Asia, Afghanistan, Pakistan and into the Middle and Near East. As well as the flashpoints shown, numerous recent trouble spots could be added — for example, the civil war in Sri Lanka, the unstable government in Thailand, the 'golden triangle' opium region of Laos, Cambodia and Burma.

THE OIL-RICH GULF STATES
Case study **10**

Much of the recent attention relating to emerging powers has focused on the BRICs, although the states of the Persian Gulf are also areas of growing influence. Saudi Arabia, Qatar, Bahrain, the United Arab Emirates (Dubai and Abu Dhabi) and Oman are all relatively stable, pro-Western Gulf states. Yemen, Iran, Iraq and Syria are also part of the Middle East but are either anti-Western or plagued by conflict. The Gulf states have two sources of power. First, they lie at the crossroads between Europe and Asia. The Persian Gulf is an ideal stopover on the long flight to or from Asia. Sun-tanning weather is pretty much guaranteed. Second, the Gulf has the world's most significant oil and gas reserves (Table 4.1). This gives them a very large bargaining chip when it comes to geopolitics because the world's dependency on oil is so great.

Table 4.1 *Oil and gas reserves of the 'friendly' Gulf states*

2008 BP data	Oil (billion barrels)	% of oil world reserves	Gas (trillion cubic metres)	% of gas world reserves
Kuwait	101.5	8.1	1.78	Under 1%
Qatar	27.2	2.2	25.6	14.4
Bahrain	0	0	0.09	Under 1%
UAE	97.8	7.8	6.09	3.4
Oman	5.6	0.4	0.69	Under 1%
Saudi Arabia	264.1	21.0	7.57	4.1

Oil and gas reserves help to explain the importance of Iran and Iraq. These two nations have taken up a disproportionate amount of diplomatic time over the last 30 years due to a succession of regional crises.

- The pro-Western Shah of Iran was overthrown during the Iranian Revolution in 1979. Since then, Iran has been anti-American.
- Iraq invaded Iran in 1980, leading to a conflict which lasted until 1988.
- Iran has long-held ambitions to develop nuclear power and nuclear weapons.
- Iraq invaded Kuwait in 1990, leading to the first Gulf War.
- The USA, UK and some other Western nations invaded Iraq in 2003 to rid the country of Saddam Hussein.

Oil and gas reserve data for Iran and Iraq are not reliable, but the BP Statistical Review of Energy in 2009 estimated Iran to have 16% of global natural gas reserves and 10.9% of oil reserves. Iraq is estimated to have 9% of oil reserves.

Put simply, oil and gas equal wealth. This statement seems to be increasingly true because of the recent history of oil prices (gas prices tend to mirror oil prices) shown in Figure 4.4. Having been low during the mid 1980s and most of the 1990s, oil prices began to rise in 2002–03 and quickly reached unheard-of levels. Even during the global recession in 2009, oil prices were often in the $50–70 range — far higher than anyone would have expected 5 years previously.

Figure 4.4
Average annual price of Dubai crude oil, 1974–2008

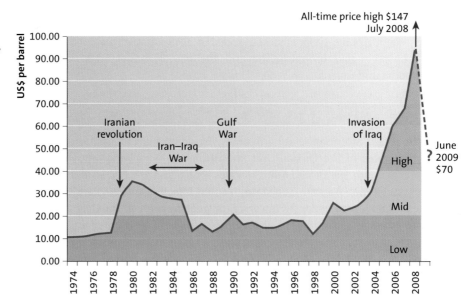

Figure 4.5
Dubai's 7-star Burj al Arab hotel

Cameron Dunn

The increasing wealth of the Gulf states has allowed them to spend as never before. Money has poured in the Gulf's direction previously — for instance, during the 1973 oil crisis, but oil price rises then were fleeting whereas recently they have been sustained. The United Arab Emirates, Qatar and Bahrain in particular have used the oil windfall:

- Each has invested heavily in creating a national flag carrier airline: Emirates in Dubai, Etihad in Abu Dhabi and Qatar Airways (see Table 4.2). These airlines, with heavily subsidised fuel, have connected the region to the wider global economy. All three focus on quality and are competing with other powerful brands such as British Airways, KLM and Singapore Airlines.
- Having created airline connections, the UAE in particular has set itself up as a luxury stopover destination and an international playground for the rich and famous. The world's first 7-star hotel, the $650 million Burj al Arab (Figure 4.5) opened in 2001.

Airport and passenger numbers, 2007	Airline HQ and expansion plans	Expansion
Dubai International — 34.4 million	Home of Emirates Airline, with a fleet of 120 planes in 2008 and 250 on order	Terminal 3 for A380 being constructed; increasing capacity to 70 million
Doha International — 10 million	Home of Qatar Airways, with a fleet of 62 planes in 2008 and 165 on order	New airport to be completed in 2015 with 90 million capacity
Abu Dhabi International — 7 million	Home of Etihad Airways, with a fleet of 26 planes in 2008 and 225 on order	Seven gates capable of handling the A380 opened in 2008, five in Terminal 3 and two in terminal 1
Al Maktoum International — a new six runway airport in the UAE with planned passenger capacity of 120 million and cargo capacity of 12 million tonnes is planned to open in 2017 and will handle foreign airlines		

Table 4.2
Airports and airlines in Qatar and the UAE

Dubai, Bahrain and Qatar have all constructed artificial islands such as the Palm and World to entice the super-rich to buy their own private beach-front property.

■ Tourism and leisure are the focus of a wider drive to diversify the Gulf economies away from their heavy dependence on oil and gas. Numerous investments are being made to attract global information technology and service TNCs. These include the $22 billion Masdar City in Abu Dhabi, a planned eco-city and science park. Dubai Internet City is an information technology park that has attracted Sony Ericsson, Microsoft and Sun Micro Systems. In Doha, Qatar, building of the $600 million Qatar Science and Technology Park began in 2009.

Aware that their place on the world stage is not guaranteed, the Gulf states have taken a lead from the existing superpowers and set up a free trade zone, similar to NAFTA and the EU single market. GAFTA, the Greater Arab Free Trade Area, began in 2005. This is a free trade zone that includes all Middle Eastern and North African nations, with the exception of Israel and Iran. The aim of GAFTA is to make cross-border trade easier and, eventually, free from tariffs and quotas. Other aims include making business travel easier within the bloc. Blocs tend to have greater negotiating power at the World Trade Organization.

Growth and diversification of the Gulf states is based on their geographical location. The region is a potential hub as it lies between Europe, North Africa, Asia and the Caucasus. Its growth has caused some concerns. First, there is the issue of cheap labour. The artificial islands and gleaming towers of the Gulf are built by low-paid migrant workers from South Asia. Many live in camps in the desert and toil for 12-hour shifts in temperatures higher than 40°C for around £250–300 per month. Their wages are used to pay back 'transit fees', typically of £1000–2000, which they owe to labour recruiters in Pakistan, India and Bangladesh. Any spare money is sent home as remittances.

The second concern is the growing power of sovereign wealth funds. A sovereign wealth fund is a government-owned investment company. Almost all assets originate from oil and gas revenues, which are then invested around the world. The largest Gulf funds are shown in Table 4.3.

Sovereign wealth funds have been used to buy stakes in some well-known companies:

■ Abu Dhabi Investment Authority owns 5% of Citigroup, a US bank, and the Kuwait Investment Authority owns a further 6%.

■ Investment Corporation of Dubai owns 20% of the London Stock Exchange Group and 100% of Travelodge hotels.

■ Qatar Investment Authority owns 10% of Credit Suisse, a bank, and 27% of Sainsbury's.

Table 4.3
Gulf sovereign wealth funds

Country	Fund Name	Estimated value in 2009 ($ billion)
UAE — Abu Dhabi	Abu Dhabi Investment Authority	627
Saudi Arabia	SAMA Foreign Holdings	431
Kuwait	Kuwait Investment Authority	203
UAE — Dubai	Investment Corporation of Dubai	82
Qatar	Qatar Investment Authority	62
UAE — Abu Dhabi	Mubadala Development Company	15
Bahrain	Mumtalakat Holding Company	14
UAE — Abu Dhabi	International Petroleum Investment Company	14

Concerns about these investments centres on the fact that foreign governments effectively own part, or all, of companies in other countries. In some cases this might give a foreign government significant direct influence over business and economics in another country.

9

Using case studies

Question

(a) **Outline the strengths and weaknesses of the Gulf states claim for emerging power status.**
(b) **In what ways might the Gulf states become more significant global players in the future?**

Guidance

(a) The main claims are their vast oil and gas reserves. These are a source of huge wealth and their sovereign wealth funds are an important way of globalising their money and influence. Locations such as Dubai and Qatar are becoming global hubs with a concentration of wealth, elites and TNCs. Political power is much weaker; the Gulf states suffer from their small stature and populations. From military and cultural points of view, their influence is minor.

(b) Power may grow, especially as remaining oil and gas reserves are concentrated increasingly in the Persian Gulf. GAFTA, if it becomes a success, may strengthen the economic power of the region in the way the single market has for the EU. Massive investment in the global hub concept may make the UAE, Qatar and Bahrain key locations for research and development as they attract TNCs to invest.

Energy superpowers

Energy resources are a path to power and status. Demand for energy resources is huge and growing. If countries such as India and China are going to continue to grow, they will need an ever increasing supply of energy. Unless a radical, cheap, reliable, easy-to-adopt new energy technology emerges very quickly, for the foreseeable future energy means fossil fuels.

Of the three fossil fuels, oil is the most desirable because it has a higher energy density than coal and is easier to transport than natural gas. In terms of pollution, coal is the dirtiest of the three fuels. As a liquid, oil has greater flexibility in terms of transport than bulky solid coal. Table 4.4 shows the top five countries by fossil fuel reserves in 2009. Three countries, Saudi Arabia, Iran and Russia stand out as having very large reserves of at least two fossil fuels. The USA has vast coal reserves, but coal is polluting and not flexible. Over the next few decades, it is likely that the importance of countries with large fossil fuel reserves will grow.

Coal reserves (% of world total)		Oil reserves (% of world total)		Gas reserves (% of world total)	
USA	27.1	Saudi Arabia	21	Russia	23.4
Russia	17.3	Canada*	12	Iran	16
China	12.6	Iran	10.9	Qatar	13.8
India	10.2	Iraq	9.1	Turkmenistan	4.3
Australia	8.6	Kuwait	8.1	Saudi Arabia	4.1

*includes Canadian oil sands

Table 4.4
Fossil fuel superpowers

It is worth mentioning some other natural resources that are highly concentrated geographically but crucial to the modern economy:

- 33% of the world's indium reserves are in Canada; it is needed to make LCD televisions and monitors.
- 62% of the world's antimony reserves are in China; it is used in pharmaceuticals.
- 88% of the world's platinum/rhodium reserves are in South Africa; it is used in catalytic converters.
- 60% of the world's chromium reserves are in Kazakhstan; it is used for plating.
- 53% of the world's hafnium reserves are in Australia; it is used in computer chips and nuclear power plants.

These resources do bestow a certain importance on the countries that are lucky enough to have them. One mineral is not enough to create a superpower, but countries that have these resources may find making friends easy.

Case study 11   RUSSIA: ENERGY GIANT

Russia is one of the most enigmatic countries on Earth. It is the world's largest country, stretching from the Baltic Sea in Europe eastward to within 53 miles of Alaska (Figure 4.6). Contained within its sprawling land mass are over 150 different ethnic groups and 100 languages are spoken. Internationally, the West has had difficulty dealing with Russia for hundreds of years:

- In the nineteenth century, Russia expanded its boundaries as an imperial power. The Russian empire was contiguous, whereas other European empires consisted of dispersed foreign colonies.
- In 1917, the Russian revolution brought the communist USSR (Union of Soviet Socialist Republics) into being. The USSR lasted until 1991.

Figure 4.6
The USSR and Russia

- During the Second World War, the USSR fought initially alongside Hitler, but following the German invasion in 1941 the USSR fought as an ally of the UK and USA.

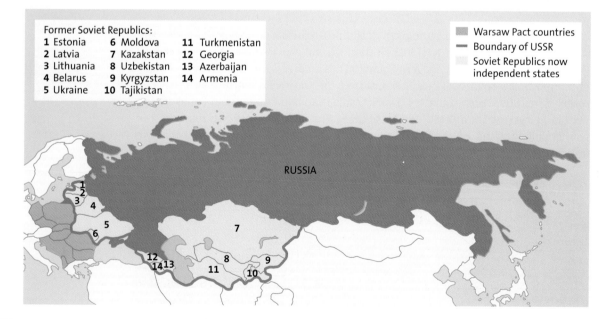

Former Soviet Republics:
1 Estonia   6 Moldova   11 Turkmenistan
2 Latvia   7 Kazakstan 12 Georgia
3 Lithuania 8 Uzbekistan 13 Azerbaijan
4 Belarus   9 Kyrgyzstan 14 Armenia
5 Ukraine   10 Tajikistan

Warsaw Pact countries
Boundary of USSR
Soviet Republics now independent states

RUSSIA

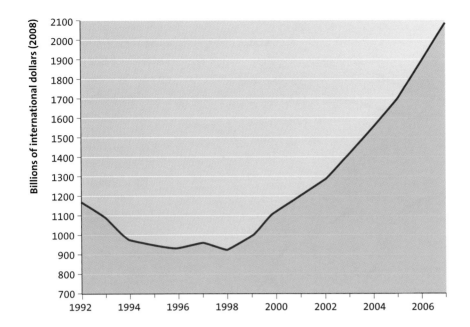

Figure 4.7
Russian GDP since the collapse of the USSR

■ 1945 ushered in the Cold War era; essentially 45 years of tense standoff between the capitalist West and the communist East. Following the collapse and break up of the USSR (see Figure 4.6), the country reverted to its old name, Russia.

In western Europe and North America the concept of democracy is the accepted political system. In Russia, much greater importance is placed on a strong leader — Russian elections today might best be described as a 'one-party democracy'. This difference seems to stem from centuries of tsarist rule (tsar roughly translates as 'emperor') followed by the leadership of strong dictators (Lenin, Stalin) during the USSR years.

Russia's resurgence as a BRIC country, and emerging power, has been under the leadership of Vladimir Putin. Putin was elected President of Russia in 2000 and served two 4-year terms. During this time, he pursued a fairly assertive foreign policy. The economy has been liberalised and has grown rapidly (Figure 4.7). In 2008, Putin had to step down because the Russian constitution allows a president to serve only two consecutive terms. Putin is serving as Prime Minister from 2008 to 2012. The new president, Dmitry Medvedev is widely seen as a front man, with Putin still in real control.

Russia's claim to be an emerging power is based on its gas reserves. These have brought great wealth to Russia and allowed it to assert its power within Europe. Reliance on Russian gas in Europe is high. Gas export pipelines pass through former Soviet republics such as Ukraine and Belarus. In 2006 and 2009, gas supplies to Ukraine were cut off over payment and price disputes, causing supplies in France and Germany to drop by 20–30%. The planned Nord Stream pipeline (Figure 4.8) should increase security of supply in northern Europe, but the planned South Stream and Nabucco pipelines run through politically troubled areas. Europe's fear is that Russia will be able to 'name its price' for gas and use gas supplies as a geopolitical weapon.

Russia has used its energy power to reassert what it calls its 'privileged sphere of influence'. In 2008, President Medvedev said: 'Russia, like other countries in the world, has regions where it has privileged interests. These are regions where countries with which we have friendly relations are located.' This was essentially warning other

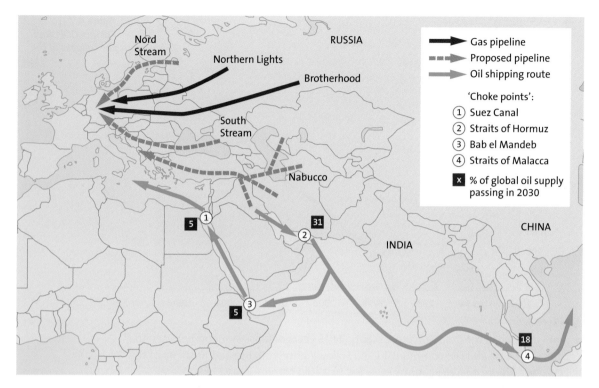

Figure 4.8
Russian gas supplies to Europe

countries to keep off what Russia considers to be its turf, i.e. the former Soviet Republics. Gas supplies have already been a source of tension and Russia also views the expansion of the EU and NATO eastwards as a threat to its regional hegemony. If Georgia and Ukraine make moves towards membership of either organisation, tension in eastern Europe would certainly increase.

To what extent does Russia deserve its status as an emerging power? Russia has some strengths but also a number of key weaknesses that might be reasons to question that it is in the same league as China.

Strengths include:

- Russia has large gas, and to a lesser extent, oil supplies, and other significant natural resources, including vast forests.
- Russia is a nuclear power, with thousands of nuclear warheads, a large navy, army and air force. This means that it is strategically important.
- Russia has a permanent seat on the UN Security Council and is a G8 member, which cannot be said for any other BRIC. This gives it the ability to influence global policy.

Weaknesses include:

- It has a political system influenced by oligarchs. These are millionaires and billionaires who snapped up chunks of Russian state-owned business, particularly gas fields, after the collapse of the USSR. Their influence on politicians may undermine the political process.
- Russia's economy is overly dependent on oil and gas exports, which account for 20% of GDP. During the 2008–09 financial crisis, the Russian stock market and currency (the ruble) both came under extreme pressure. The Russian trading system stock index fell by 54% in 2008 and falls were so steep that the stock market was often closed to prevent a complete collapse in share prices.

- Russia has an ageing population. Combined with a health crisis (AIDS, alcoholism, heart disease), this led to sharply falling total population in the decade from 1996 to 2006. The falls have stabilised but the long-term future is unclear.
- Russia is seen as a difficult place to do business. In 2006, foreign investment was around one-fiftieth of that which flowed into China.

A *New York Times* article in 2006 stated 'BIC, not BRIC, is the better formula. Call them the "breakout industrialising countries". Russia is quite out of place with that crowd.' (*NY Times*, 7 February 2006). This view reflects the fact that Russia is not industrialising and developing a diversified economy. It simply sells oil and gas, and its economic power is too closely linked to the oil price.

BRAZIL, THE REGIONAL POWER

Case study 12

In 2008, Brazil had the tenth largest economy in the world. It is a nation of false dawns — repeatedly threatening to break into the economic big league, then falling back. Figure 4.9 shows the course of Brazil's total GDP since 1960. Brazil's growth pattern for 40 years has been one of rapid accelerations followed by sharp downturns. This lack of stable, sustained growth is not characteristic of a superpower. Brazil has experienced a number of different periods of growth, stagnation and decline in the past few decades.

Slow growth during the 1960s resulted partly from a military coup in 1964, which overthrew the democratic government. This military leadership lasted until 1985. The economy grew steadily from the late 1960s as the country industrialised, developing industries such as car manufacturing as a result of foreign investment by companies such as Fiat and VW. At the time, Brazil was an attractive low-wage economy. Inflation and debt grew steadily during this period. By the early 1980s, Brazil's **foreign debt** exceeded $100 billion and high oil prices had slowed growth. In the years after 1979, the Brazilian government was forced by the International Monetary Fund to cut spending in an attempt to control growing debts. Throughout the 1980s and 1990s high inflation eroded economic progress.

Only in 1994, with the introduction of the economic *plano real* was inflation defeated. This pegged the Brazilian currency, the real, to the US dollar. Once well over 1000% per year, inflation fell to 23% in 1995. Since then the Brazilian economy has grown,

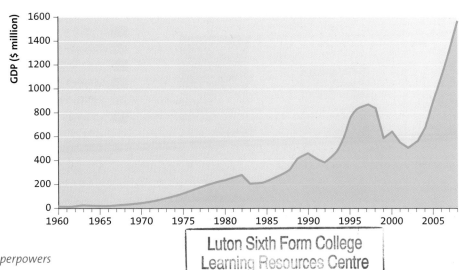

Figure 4.9
Brazilian GDP, 1960–2008

Economic sectors, 2007–08 (% of GDP)	Agriculture	Industry	Services
EU	2.1	27.3	70.5
Brazil	5.5	28.7	65.8
China	11.3	48.6	40.1
Russia	4.6	39.1	56.3
India	17.2	29.1	53.7

Table 4.5
Economic sectors in the EU and BRICs

but much more slowly than those of the other BRICs. Whereas China and India have achieved annual economic growth of 8–12% since the early 1990s, growth of 3–4% is more typical of Brazil.

Compared with the other BRICs, Brazil is, in some ways, more like a developed country. As Table 4.5 shows, the proportion of GDP from the three main economic sectors is closer to the EU than any of the other BRICs. This suggests that Brazil has a mature, consumer-driven economy.

Perhaps the slow and steady progress of Brazil is beginning to pay off. The TNC Fiat first invested in Brazil in 1976, but concerns over inflation, rising wages and debt prevented further investment. Encouraged by the anti-inflation *plano real*, Fiat invested over $1 billion in its Betim factory in 1996. Fiat's strategy was to build a small car, the Palio, to sell to Brazil's growing middle class. This approach to foreign direct investment was more about a growing local market than cheap wages to produce for export. By 2009, Fiat had produced 10 million cars in Brazil.

Fiat's strategy has paid off because the number of middle-class consumers in Brazil has grown in recent years. Figure 4.10 shows how middle-income groups in Brazil grew between 2000 and 2005; the number of people earning under $3000 per year fell. The proportion of Brazilians living below the poverty line fell from 35% in 1992 to 23% by 2005. Numbers in the $$5900–22 000 earning bracket swelled significantly.

This increasing number of consumers, with aspirations for home and car ownership, has been a significant force in the Brazilian economy over the last decade.

Brazil has other strengths. In the 1960s and 1970s, Brazil was heavily reliant on oil imports. The 1973 oil crisis, with its quadrupling of the oil price, was a severe shock to the country. Brazil embarked on a major programme to reduce dependency on

Figure 4.10
The growing Brazilian middle class

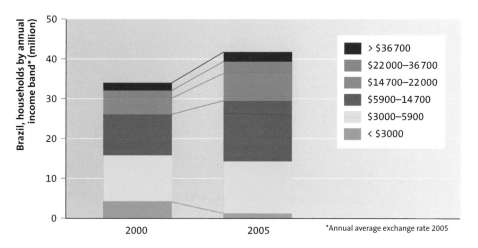

imported oil by replacing it with home-produced ethanol made from sugar cane. If there is one thing Brazil does not lack, it is land. This meant that sugar cane could be grown without converting food-producing farms to biofuel production. In 1975, the National Alcohol Programme was launched. This aimed to shift vehicles away from petrol to ethanol:

- Normal petrol-engined cars can run with 5–10% of petrol being replaced by ethanol, but different engines are required to run on pure ethanol (often called E100).
- Ford, Fiat and VW all began to produce cars in Brazil that could run on various blends of petrol and ethanol, and E100.
- In 1993, a national standard of E22 was set as the minimum percentage of ethanol in the fuel mix. Pure petrol is no longer sold in Brazil.
- By 1990, one-third of all vehicles in Brazil were running on the E100 fuel, considerably reducing Brazil's need to import oil. The size of the market encouraged car manufacturers to develop cars that could run on any mix of petrol and ethanol — so-called 'flex-fuel' cars. Brazil has been at the forefront of biofuel development for over 30 years, and is well placed to take advantage of the global interest in biofuels that has recently emerged.
- By 2008, ethanol accounted for around 50% of all fuel used in cars in Brazil, and 20% of total road transport fuel — around 4.5 billion gallons and second only to ethanol production in the USA.

Ironically, since the 1970s, oil exploration has increased Brazil's known oil reserves. Production has risen from around 180 000 barrels per day to over 2 million barrels per day. Brazil is now self-sufficient in liquid fuels because of its farsighted move into ethanol and lucky discovery of large oil reserves — amounting to some 12 billion barrels in 2008.

Brazil has a number of world-class companies. Embraer, a government-owned aircraft maker privatised in 1994, has become a leader in the regional jet market. It is the world's fourth largest maker of commercial jets behind Boeing (USA), Airbus (France) and Bombardier (Canada). Embraer has a workforce of 20 000 in a highly advanced industrial sector. In 2009, Embraer had around $20 billion worth of orders on its books, ranging from 90–110-seater regional jets to 3–4-seater executive aircraft.

Regional power?

Does Brazil have the credentials to be classed as an emerging power and potential superpower? There are several factors against its claim:

- Politics and democracy in Brazil are relatively young, and **populism** still plays a role in politics. This tends to detract from rational economic policies and long-term planning. Politics in Brazil tends to be personality, not policy, driven and corrupt politicians are common.
- Crime is a major problem. In 2007, the annual murder rate was 25 per 100 000 people, compared with six in the USA and around two in the UK. Crime has generated fear and gated communities, and may put off some foreign investment.
- Education lags far behind both the developed world and competitors such as China. The average person of working age in Brazil has 4 years of schooling compared with 6 years in China. Of the 37 OECD-plus-partner countries, Brazilian 15-year-olds scored last in science ability in 2008 (*Education at a Glance 2008: OECD Indicators*).
- Brazil is a bureaucratic country with a 'big' government. This means doing business can be complex and time consuming. In the World Bank's 2009 *Ease of Doing Business*

report Brazil came 125th — behind Bangladesh and Ethiopia and way short of the USA (3rd), the UK (6th) and communist China (83rd).

On a more positive note Brazil does have several strong points:

- It is beginning to enter the international stage. Brazil is a member if the G8+5, which is a dialogue between the G8, BRICs and Mexico. Brazil could gain a permanent UN Security Council seat if membership expands.
- Brazil is self-sufficient in energy, timber and many mineral resources. It is sometimes described as an 'agricultural superpower'. There may be up to 350 million hectares of potential farmland in Brazil with only 70–80 in use today. Food exports are a major earner, with Brazil producing around 15% of the world's food but having only 3% of the world's population.
- Brazil has played a key role in increased South American integration. This culminated in 2008 with the launch of the Union of South America (UNASUL), modelled on the EU. UNASUL aims to give the region a more powerful global voice. It is still in its infancy but is aims are far reaching:
  - a Bank of the South to help finance development in the region, set up in 2007
  - a single market and free trade between member states, to be implemented by 2014 for some products and 2019 for all products
  - cooperation over infrastructure planning, especially road and energy projects
  - 90-day visitor visas that need only an identity card to obtain, to allow freer movement of people
  - work towards a common defence policy

As the key regional economic power, it was perhaps not surprising that the UNASUL agreement was signed into life in Brasilia, capital of Brazil, in 2008.

Mexico: not a BRIC?

Mexico was not included in the original BRIC group of emerging powers. In some ways this is a strange omission. A 2008 report by the accountancy and consulting group Grant Thornton entitled *Emerging Markets: Reshaping the Global Economy* ranked the emerging economies using a range of measures of economic and wider development. These measures included the human development index (HDI), GDP, population, imports and exports and foreign direct investment (FDI). The results are shown in Figure 4.11. These results might be seen as undermining the BRIC concept because Mexico comes out ahead of Brazil. The index does confirm that China is significantly ahead of any of the other BRICS. Mexico does well because:

- it has a relatively high GDP per capita ($11 500 in 2008)
- it is a major oil exporter, although its oil exports appear to have peaked
- like Brazil, it has a large middle class that is beginning to consume goods at similar levels to those seen in parts of Europe

Another obvious strength is that Mexico has close ties to the USA. It is part of the North American Free Trade Agreement (NAFTA), which has allowed it to benefit from tariff-free imports and exports to the USA and Canada. Mexico has become a major location for FDI from the USA, as US companies seek to reduce costs by locating production there.

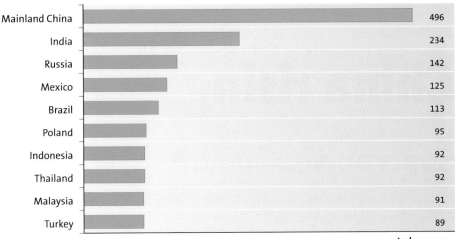

	Index score
Mainland China	496
India	234
Russia	142
Mexico	125
Brazil	113
Poland	95
Indonesia	92
Thailand	92
Malaysia	91
Turkey	89

Figure 4.11
The 2008 Grant Thornton emerging markets index (higher scores indicate greater potential for future economic growth)

Mexico does have a number of weaknesses:

- Despite being a relatively stable democracy, it has high levels of crime and corruption.
- Economic policy has tended to lead to 'boom and bust' in Mexico and it has had difficulties with its foreign debt.
- Few Mexican companies are world-beaters and it may be over-reliant on FDI at the expense of building up its own industries.

Goldman Sachs left Mexico out of the original BRIC group based on the fact that as a country it was already well developed and lacked the future potential for growth of the other BRICs.

10 Using case studies

Question

(a) To what extent does Russia have superpower potential and what factors could destabilise the country?

(b) What evidence is there that Brazil is a 'regional leader'?

Guidance

(a) Russia's potential is as an energy superpower as it has large gas reserves. In addition, it still has the nuclear and military technology legacy from when the USSR was a superpower. Culturally, and in a wider economic sense, Russia is quite weak and lacks influence. There are numerous sources of instability including its political system, collapse in demand for its oil and gas (unlikely), its troublesome border regions and conflict between former Soviet Republics that are now independent nations. Longer term, its ageing population is a concern.

(b) Brazil's case to be a BRIC is not particularly strong. However, it has played a leading role in the regional integration of South America through UNASUL. It is a technological leader in terms of biofuels and some areas of manufacturing, such as aircraft. It could be the bread-basket of Latin America with its huge land areas.

Part 4

China rising

Superpower, again?

China is very much the country of the moment. A strong case could be made for viewing China as the world's most important nation as it takes the number one spot in 2009 by several measures:

- the world's most populous country, with over 1.3 billion people
- the world's biggest emitter of greenhouse gases
- the world's largest army, at 2.3 million soldiers
- the world's largest number of landlines, mobile phones and internet users
- the world's largest manufacturing production

To students of Chinese economic history these superlatives might seem to mark a return to superpower status. Prior to 1600, China and India were the world's largest economies. During the Qing dynasty, some estimates suggest China's economy accounted for one-third of global economic activity. China's star began to dim in the nineteenth century with the rise of Britain as an industrial and imperial power. China's economic and political history up to the late 1970s is briefly outlined in Table 5.1.

Table 5.1
China's economic and political history

Date	Politics	Economics
1839–42 and 1856–60 Anglo-Chinese opium wars	Conflict over trade rights led to two wars with Britain both of which China lost; Britain becomes the hegemonic power in SE Asia	China is forced to open up to European trade, including trade in the drug opium
1851–1873 Internal rebellion	A series of civil wars, related to religion and clan rivalries undermined the power of dynastic rule and led to millions of deaths	The opium trade, and the effects of the drug on people, crime and trade increased China's reliance on foreign powers
1894–95 Sino-Japanese war	War between Japan and China, which contributed to Japan's status as the regional power	China lost control of Korea and Taiwan
1899–1901 Boxer Rebellion	Boxers were anti-foreign, anti-Christian rebels who attempted to drive the Western powers out of China; they were defeated, but China was forced to pay reparations to Japan, Russia, the UK, USA and the other countries that put down the rebellion	China was almost colonised during this period; China becomes heavily reliant on imported European goods
1911 Revolution	Qing dynasty overthrown leading to the formation of a republic. This was a highly unstable period	Economic stagnation, famine and hyperinflation
1937 Invasion	Japanese invade China and rule it until 1945	The economy of China virtually grinds to a standstill under Japanese rule
1945–1949 Civil war	Communists under Mao Zedong and the Nationalist Kuomintang under Chang Kai-Shek fight a devastating civil war	By 1949, the Chinese economy had been 'at war' for over 12 years

In 1949, the Communists were victorious and founded the People's Republic of China (PRC). Chinese nationalists fled to Taiwan. To this day 'China' is a divided nation. The People's Republic of China (mainland) and the Republic of China (Taiwan) maintain a strained relationship. No major power (or the UN) officially recognises Taiwan as a 'country' because the PRC refuses to have any diplomatic relations with any country that does. However, Taiwan is economically and politically supported by the West.

China (PRC) remained an insular, isolated nation throughout the 1950s and 1960s. China and the USSR, another communist nation and seemingly natural ally, did not cooperate with each other. The two countries had very different forms of communism because China was a rural nation and the USSR was increasingly urban and industrial. Modern China, and the origins of the economic powerhouse of today, can be dated to economic reforms instigated by Premier Deng Xiaoping in 1978.

WHY CHINA?

Case study 13

Since China's economic reforms its progress has been remarkable (Figure 5.1). Purchasing power GDP per capita has seen uninterrupted growth from $250 to nearly $6000 in less than 30 years. The proportion of Chinese in poverty (living on less than $1.25 per day) has fallen from over 60% to under 10%. In a generation China has been transformed from a rural agricultural country to an urban industrial one. Some estimates suggest that in 2008 there were upwards of 800 000 millionaires in China.

China's economic growth results from a number of interrelated factors:

■ Economic reforms begun in 1978 — most importantly an 'open door' policy towards foreign direct investment (FDI) which encouraged TNCs to locate manufacturing plants in China.

■ Setting up of special economic zones (free trade, or export processing, zones) beginning with Shenzhen on the Pearl River Delta in 1980. There are now dozens of these. All have various forms of low taxes, open import–export systems, an export orientation, and limited regulations on labour, e.g. non-union or no-strike agreements.

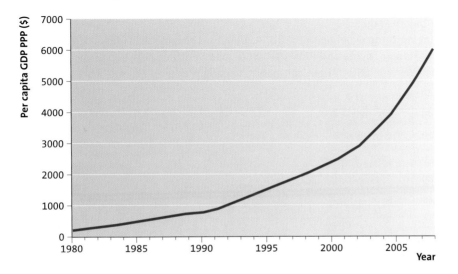

Figure 5.1
Chinese per capita GDP growth since 1980

- the size of the local market in China has become increasingly important since 2000 as the Chinese themselves have become consumers, reducing the reliance on exports. In addition, geographical proximity to large Asian markets has helped exports.
- a huge pool of low-wage but highly skilled and motivated labour. Chinese education is the country's trump card. The literacy rate in 2008 was 92%. Around 20% of students go on to higher education whereas only 1% did in 1978. There are more undergraduates in China than there are people in Australia.
- a focus on exports that undercut MEDC prices. In some cases, this has involved direct copying of foreign products and ideas; in others, joint ventures with Western TNCs have filled technology gaps.
- huge investment in infrastructure (ports, roads, airports, telecommunications and energy) by the PRC government — for instance, $250 billion were invested in roads between 1990 and 2005, with plans to build 80 000 km of motorways in the next 20 years.

China has also been lucky enough to grow in an era of globalisation. Internet and satellite communications have increasingly 'shrunk' the perceived distance to China from Europe and North America and allowed TNCs to keep in touch with far-flung factories. Transport costs, especially air travel and container shipping, have fallen in the last two decades. This has benefited China's export-oriented economy.

FDI explains much of China's economic growth. Until recently, 70% of this was in the manufacturing sector. In 2003, over 40 000 firms invested in China, with companies from Taiwan, USA, Japan, South Korea and Europe all big investors. As Figure 5.2 shows, China has taken by far the largest FDI slice of any of the BRIC nations. FDI is not all good news. While foreign-owned factories provide jobs, few taxes are paid in free trade zones and profits leak out of China back to the home countries of the TNCs. Local suppliers benefit from contracts, but technology is not transferred.

For China to become a global player it needs to develop its own industries and own innovation. The car industry illustrates how China is attempting to do this. In 2008, China made more cars than any other country — just over 9 million (2 million in 2000). Can you name a Chinese car company? Probably not, but several, for example Geely, Chery, SAIC and Dongfeng are growing rapidly. China's car industry has gone through a number of stages:

- **Joint ventures** — between 1980 and 2000 most cars made in China, such as Shanghai GM, Tianjin Toyota and FAW-VW, were joint ventures between Chinese companies and Western TNCs. These companies usually produced old models from the West.

Figure 5.2
FDI in the BRICs

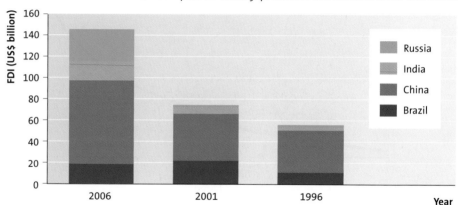

Contemporary Case Studies

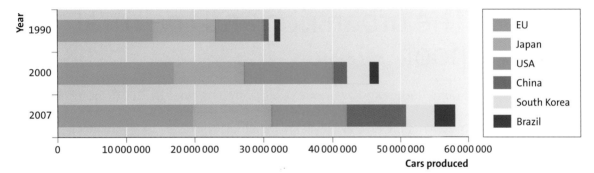

Shanghai Volkswagen Automotive still produces the Santana based on a VW Passat first sold in Europe in 1981. Virtually all technology was imported to China.

- **Indigenous producers** — in the late 1990s local companies began to build cars on their own. Geely produced its first car in 1998 and Chery in 1999. Chery were sued in 2004 by GM for copying the Daewoo Matiz. This fairly blatant 'borrowing' of Western design and technology has been common but has allowed rapid commercial development of models.
- **Innovation** — from around 2005, Chinese companies began developing their own designs and products, evidence that the industry is maturing and eyeing export markets. At the Shanghai Auto Show in 2009 numerous Chinese manufacturers exhibited concept cars.

Figure 5.3
Changing car production, 1990–2007

The stunning rise of China's car industry can be seen in Figure 5.3. Between 2000 and 2007, car production in the EU, USA and Japan remained relatively stable; in the emerging countries of South Korea and Brazil it doubled. In China, production quadrupled in 7 years, whereas in the USA it fell by around 20%.

Dramatic changes in car production have led to dramatic rises in car ownership in China, creating a more mobile, consumer society. China's citizens have grabbed onto some technologies with both hands. By 2008 there were 220 million internet users, more than in the USA. Mobile phone numbers grew from 87 million in 2000 to 430 million in 2008.

11 Using case studies

Question
(a) Outline the reasons for China's recent rapid economic growth.
(b) How important has FDI been to China's recent success?

Guidance
(a) These reasons might usefully be grouped. First, there are the political and economic reforms of the late 1970s and increased openness to the rest of the world. Human resources — a well-educated, low-wage workforce of seemingly limitless size — have allowed industry to grow. Government policies such as infrastructure investment and free trade zones have played an important role, and been copied in other countries. The increasing wealth of the Chinese has created an internal market that has recently become a crucial source of continued growth.
(b) FDI has been vital — it was the reason that growth in jobs and exports began. However, you should consider whether it is as important now, given the growth in Chinese TNCs and home-grown industrial development and markets.

The urban rich and the rural poor

Income inequality has grown significantly in China. By 2007, the richest 10% enjoyed 45% of all the income whereas the poorest 10% shared only 1.4%. The majority of the rich, including around 60 billionaires in 2007 (according to *Forbes* magazine), are urban. Rampant urbanisation has created a new, consumerist middle class — particularly in the service sector, as demand for lawyers, accountants and PR people has grown. However, China's Gini coefficient of inequality rose from 0.31 to 0.44 over the 1980–2001 period as inequality grew.

Most of the poor in China are rural, but they are rarer than they were. Globalisation and the economic miracle have reduced poverty levels in a way that most countries envy. The total number of rural poor (living on under $1 per day) has fallen from around 250 million in 1978 to around 30 million in 2006. Despite this huge achievement, there is little in the way of trickle-down to rural areas — most young rural people simply migrate to urban areas, creating a growing problem of rural ageing. There are still some 700 million rural farm workers in China. This has created a stark divide between coastal urban wealth and interior rural poverty (Figures 5.4 and 5.5). One significant problem is rural land-grabbing, by the state and private companies, for infrastructure, suburban homes and new factories. A total of 6.5 million hectares of farmland have been lost in the last 20 years. Rural people whose land is taken often do not receive compensation. It is important to recognise that not everyone has benefited from China's growth and it is very much a country of 'haves' and 'have nots'.

Figure 5.4
Many Chinese people struggle to make a living

Fotolia

Contemporary Case Studies

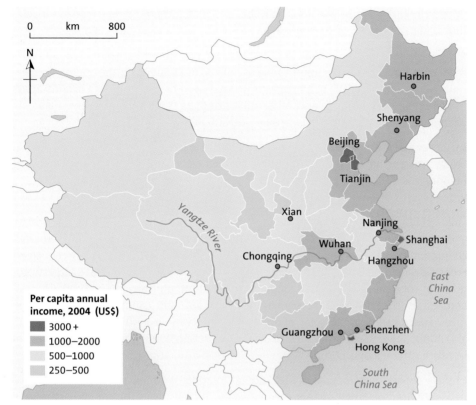

Figure 5.5
Income inequality in China

Per capita annual income, 2004 (US$)
- 3000 +
- 1000–2000
- 500–1000
- 250–500

The environmental payback

A significant threat to China's continued growth is the health of its environment. Three days before the opening ceremony of the 2008 Beijing Olympics the city's Air Pollution Index was measured at 91. By World Health Organization standards a reading of 50 + is considered 'high' and 100 + as unsafe. Beijing's dirty air came close to derailing the Olympic dream. This was despite huge efforts to clean up Beijing before the athletes arrived:

- 1300 petrol stations were upgraded to sell cleaner fuels
- vehicles failing to meet strict new emissions standards were banned from Beijing
- 50% of the city's 3.3 million cars were banned from driving every day
- some factories were forced to shut during the Olympics

Beijing did succeed, but nine of the ten most polluted cities in the world are in China. Acid precipitation falls on 30% of the country. According to the World Bank, air pollution costs the Chinese economy $25 billion a year in health costs and lost productivity. A World Health Organization Report in 2007 found that urban air pollution kills 656 000 Chinese every year and polluted water kills a further 95 000. Ninety per cent of urban waterways and lakes are severely polluted and major pollution incidents are becoming more common. In 2005, an explosion at a petrochemical factory in Jilin city released nitrobenzene into the Songhua River forcing the shutdown of the water supply to Harbin, a city with a population of 3.8 million at the time. In

2008, tributaries of the Han River in Hubei province turned red due to pollution, cutting water supplies to 200 000 people.

More worrying still is evidence that the dash for growth and quick profits puts consumers at direct risk. The 2008 Chinese milk scandal involved the chemical melamine being added to milk to increase its protein content. This was sold to consumers in a number of baby-milk and other milk products. The polluted milk caused six child deaths, and may have made over 300 000 people ill.

Incidents like these show that public health and the health of the wider environment are at risk as Chinese economic growth rushes on, but regulatory frameworks lag behind.

Green means growth?

China's environmental track record is worrying. However, it is likely to see environmental concern as much as an opportunity as a threat. Investing in green, clean technology can create jobs and exports. In 2009, China was the world's largest producer of solar panels, with 25% of global production, up from 8% in 2005. Chinese companies like Suntech have scaled up production, and exports, and at the same time reduced the cost of solar photovoltaic panels by around 50% between 2007 and 2009. Suntech exported 98% of its solar panels in 2008, undercutting producers in North America and Europe.

China's dependency on coal is well known. In 2006, it added around 70 000 MW of new coal-fired electricity generating capacity. Increasingly, these new coal plants are using clean coal technology to extract a greater useful percentage of power from coal, reducing the increase in overall emissions. China is rapidly becoming the world leader in clean coal technology.

China doubled its installed wind power capacity every year between 2004 and 2008. Should wind power growth continue at this rate, China will meet its target of 30 000 MW of wind power by 2020 10 years early.

Uniquely, China seems able to harness its vast industrial capacity to meet targets and undertake seismic policy shifts. It seems likely that emerging green technologies will be rapidly perfected by Chinese manufacturers and exported to the world, creating jobs and profits for China and perhaps more environmentally sustainable solutions for the planet.

Is the strain beginning to show?

There are pressures inside China that could yet derail its dash for superpower status. When the first economic reforms were made in 1978 only 170 million Chinese were urban. By 2008, that number had grown to 570 million. This has placed huge strain on cities to house new residents, most of whom are migrants. There are other pressures:

- **Energy** — just keeping pace with energy demand, to power the factories, meant that China had to open two new coal-fired power stations every 10 days between 2005 and 2008; coal demand doubled from 1990 to 2007.
- **Water** — northern China is dry, but increasingly urban and industrial. Around 60% of China's cities, including Beijing, are short of water. Two-thirds of water comes from groundwater aquifers, most of which are over-pumped.
- **Ageing** — China faces a dramatically ageing future. The success of its one-child policy in controlling birth rate has created a greying population with 17% of Chinese expected to be over 60 by 2020. This will increase healthcare, pensions and housing costs. It also reduces the availability of young, innovative workers and could create skills shortages.
- **Freedom** — political freedom is limited by the Chinese Communist Party. Free elections, free speech and other rights do not exist in China. Demands for these rights reached crisis point in Tiananmen Square, Beijing in 1989 when student protests were met with a brutal clampdown by the army and police. Estimates suggest somewhere between 200 and 3000 people died. A re-run of this type of protest could destabilise China.
- **Economy** — the global recession of 2007–09 showed that China was vulnerable. Exports in May 2009 were 26% lower than the year before and thousands of factories closed and perhaps 20 million factory workers lost their jobs.

The Chinese government introduced a $600 billion economic stimulus plan to keep the economy growing at 6% per year — the figure economists estimated was necessary to prevent social unrest.

China's strengths as a growing economy are not in doubt, but it does have a number of weaknesses that it will need to overcome before it rises to the number one spot so many people seem to anticipate.

Using case studies

12

Question
Assess the costs of the Chinese economic miracle, for both human and ecosystem wellbeing.

Guidance
Your answer should consider human health and pollution, inequality and poverty and the degree to which industrialisation has sacrificed other aspects of Chinese lifestyle. Pollution and ecosystem degradation are also serious issues that need careful consideration. Move towards a conclusion by asking yourself if the costs have been worth it for the majority of Chinese.

CHINA'S AFRICAN ADVENTURE

Case study **14**

Since 2000, China has changed direction and begun investing abroad. This is especially the case in Africa (Figure 5.6). China is seeking to secure resources, oil primarily, but also minerals, ores and timber. FDI from China to Africa rose dramatically from $75 million in 2003 to $400 million by 2005. By 2007, total investment had ballooned to $30 billion. Trade has followed the same pattern, rising by 45% between 2007 and

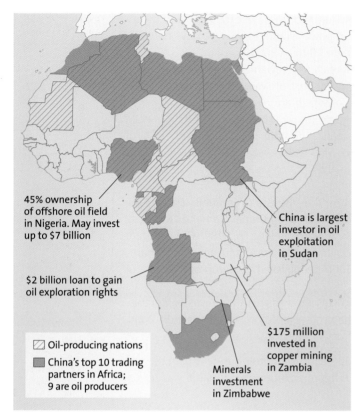

45% ownership of offshore oil field in Nigeria. May invest up to $7 billion

$2 billion loan to gain oil exploration rights

China is largest investor in oil exploitation in Sudan

$175 million invested in copper mining in Zambia

Minerals investment in Zimbabwe

Oil-producing nations

China's top 10 trading partners in Africa; 9 are oil producers

Figure 5.6
China in Africa

2008 to $109 billion. Chinese exports to Africa accounted for $51 billion, and imports to China reached $58 billion. In the next few years, China is set to top the USA as Africa's biggest trading partner.

Around 30% of all oil used in China comes from Africa. Critics argue that all China wants from Africa is its resources, and that it has no interest in African development. Most investment money either goes to African governments, TNCs and Chinese companies, not to ordinary Africans. China has been accused of overlooking human rights issues. In many cases, large Chinese-funded infrastructure projects are built by Chinese workers, not local labour. There were an estimated 750 000 Chinese working in Africa in 2008, and over 900 Chinese companies.

China's involvement in Sudan has been the subject of intense debate. The Greater Nile Oil Pipeline, opened in 1999 and stretching nearly 1000 miles from the southern Sudan oil fields to Port Sudan, is 40% owned by China National Petroleum Corporation (CNPC). The oil refinery at Port Sudan is 50% owned by CNPC. Some 60–80% of Sudan's 500 000–700 000 barrels per day oil production is thought to go to China in a deal worth perhaps $2 billion per year to Sudan.

Figure 5.7 shows how oil concessions (the rights to explore, drill and extract) have been carved up in Sudan, and the dominance of Chinese companies.

China has essentially filled a vacuum left when increasing violence in Darfur, western Sudan, drove some Western countries away. Some have argued that an unstable Sudan protects China's interests by keeping competitors out. In the run up to the 2008 Beijing Olympics, there were protests against China's economic support for Sudan — Steven Spielberg and Mia Farrow protested at what they called China's support for Sudan's genocide in Darfur. China has done deals elsewhere in Africa:

- In Angola in 2004, China secured future oil supplies with $2 billion in loans and aid, which included money for Chinese companies to build hospitals, bridges, schools, roads, and lay a telephone network, as well as train Angolan workers to maintain it.
- NCFA, a Chinese company, has invested in several Zambian copper mines, including Chambishi and Luanshya. Copper is a key industrial metal.

These investments bring both costs and benefits to the countries concerned, as is summarised in Table 5.2.

In 2007, the *Guardian* reported on Chinese Premier Hu Jintao's eight-nation tour of Africa. Hu cancelled his plans to visit a new Chinese-funded copper smelter in Zambia because workers were protesting over working conditions. He would also have faced

Contemporary Case Studies

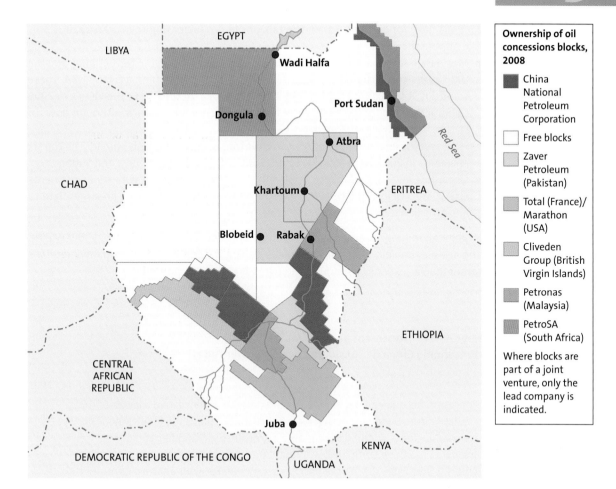

Figure 5.7
Oil concessions in Sudan, 2008 (based on Sudanese Petroleum Corporation data)

Ownership of oil concessions blocks, 2008

- China National Petroleum Corporation
- Free blocks
- Zaver Petroleum (Pakistan)
- Total (France)/ Marathon (USA)
- Cliveden Group (British Virgin Islands)
- Petronas (Malaysia)
- PetroSA (South Africa)

Where blocks are part of a joint venture, only the lead company is indicated.

demonstrations from redundant workers from the Mulungushi textile mill in Kabwe, which closed in 2007 as imported Chinese textiles undercut its prices. Ironically the 1000-worker factory was opened in 1983 with around £11 million of Chinese money. The Chinese invested more money and technical assistance in 1997–98 and took a 66% ownership stake in the textile factory. The factory may reopen if new investment can be found but it would need to be able to compete on both price and quality.

It remains to be seen whether the financial benefits of such investment help some of Africa's least developed countries out of poverty. Critics argue that China is simply creating dependency, and interfering in much the same way that Europe and North

Table 5.2
Costs and benefits of Chinese investment in Africa

Benefits	Costs
Jobs are created in major infrastructure projects funded by Chinese investment	The skilled jobs, and even some unskilled, are actually filled by imported Chinese labour
China provides Africa with much needed aid as part of investment deals	Much of the aid is tied: it is spent on Chinese equipment made by Chinese companies
Chinese factories bring modern working practices to Africa	Chinese factories undercut indigenous firms on cost, forcing them to close
China has modernised resource extraction and increased productivity and exports	Raw material exports still dominate and these are prone to price fluctuations

America have for decades. For all the talk of China's increasing role in Africa, it is only one player among many:

■ Most FDI in Africa originates from Europe, especially France, the Netherlands and the UK. South Africa is a major investor in other African economies, as is the USA. These countries still account for over 50% of FDI to Africa. According to the OECD, in 2008 China accounted for less than 1% of the total stock of FDI in Africa, although flows of FDI are rising rapidly.

■ FDI goes to a small number of African countries — it is not evenly spread. The top six recipients in 2007 were Nigeria, Egypt, South Africa, Morocco, Libya and Sudan.

■ China has invested relatively small sums in Africa compared with its investments elsewhere. FDI into the USA, Russia, South Korea and Australia are all larger than to any African nation.

In general, mining, quarrying and forestry bring few skilled jobs and pay low wages. The age-old problem of Africa's resources leaving the continent as cheap raw materials rather than as expensive manufactured goods is likely to continue.

13 Using case studies

Question

(a) On balance, is Chinese investment good or bad for Sudan?

(b) To what extent should China be considered a superpower today?

Guidance

(a) You should approach this question by examining the positive and negative aspects of the Sudan–China relationship. Sudan is getting a lot of investment but is the involvement purely economic? To what degree is Sudan handing over its resources to another country too cheaply? China's role has been compared with that of a colonial power, but is this really fair?

(b) Return to Figure 1.1 and Table 2.1. These provide a structure for your answer. Consider the four pillars in Figure 1.1 and the extent to which China has these. Table 2.1 should be used in combination with other information from the China chapter to make a judgement about China's current status. There is no doubt that China is the strongest BRIC, but has it moved beyond this grouping?

Energised India

Bengal tiger or lumbering elephant?

India's claims on emerging power status are not as strong as those of China. India has a number of claims of which it can be proud, such as being the world's largest democracy. 700 million people were eligible to vote in the 2009 elections at 800 000 polling stations. India managed, uniquely for a large country, to tread a path between the Cold War superpowers of the USA and USSR and develop in its own way. India's population in 1947 — the year it gained its independence from Britain — was around 350 million. Today, its population is 1150 million. Somehow India has managed to feed its massively expanding population and avoid famine.

India's claim to be an emerging power is weakened by its level of development. Of the four BRICs, India is the least developed by almost any measure. Figure 6.1 illustrates the relationship between HDI and proportion of GDP from agriculture in 2008. HDI is a composite index of development that combines adult literacy, education level, life expectancy and average income.

Figure 6.1 shows that three of the BRICs cluster at an HDI of 0.75–0.80 and a percentage of agriculture between 5% and 12%. India is an outlier from this group. In fact, India's HDI is very similar to that of Pakistan, Morocco and Burma. Its agricultural composition is similar to Bangladesh and Vietnam. This seems to suggest that India's inclusion as a BRIC is a little tenuous. Why is it classified as a BRIC?

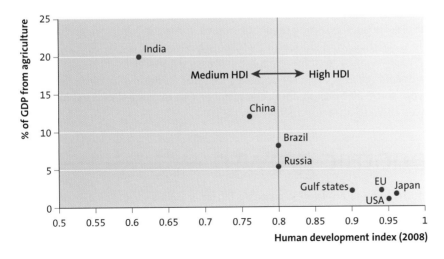

Figure 6.1
The relationship between HDI and agricultural GDP in 2008

- First, India is a demographic superpower. Its huge population, projected to be over 1.3 billion in 2025 means a very large potential market. India's population is youthful and potentially innovative and entrepreneurial.
- Second, it is a nuclear power, making it impossible to ignore. India has large and advanced armed forces — it is the only country bordering the Indian Ocean that has aircraft carriers and advanced submarines. India's space programme shows its mastery of superpower technology.
- Third, it is strategically important, and stable, in a region that has more than its fair share of difficulties. India has the potential to act as a regional power broker to calm tensions.
- Fourth, India has developed world-class services prompting Goldman Sachs to describe it as 'the back office to the world' in 2007. These services have the potential to grow.

Key to India's success is a policy U-turn implemented in the early 1990s:
- Prior to 1947, India was a colony of Britain, which restricted development.
- After 1947, India followed a path of self-sufficiency, government intervention and state economic planning. This restricted economic growth to what became known as, disparagingly, the 'Hindu rate of growth'.
- In 1991, a series of economic reforms began to open up India to world trade, FDI and economic growth.

The 1991 reforms were forced by a number of key events. Two prime ministers, Indira Gandhi and Rajiv Gandhi were assassinated in 1984 and 1991 respectively. This gave the impression of a state in chaos and deterred investment. In the 1980s, imports far exceeded exports leading to a balance of payments and debt crisis. The International Monetary Fund bailed India out, but demanded reforms:
- The Indian rupee was devalued to make exports more competitive, and imports more costly.
- A labyrinthine system of licences for importing and investment was simplified.
- State-run businesses were deregulated and some were privatised.
- Import taxes were reduced from around 80% to 25%.
- The tax system and foreign ownership of business rules were reformed.

These reforms are an example of economic **liberalisation**. They aimed to encourage free enterprise, the setting up of businesses, risk taking and foreign investment. In many ways they were similar to the Chinese reforms of 1978. Special economic zones (SEZs — similar to Chinese export processing and free trade zones) have been used to encourage FDI. India set up Asia's first SEZ in Kandla in 1965. Before 2005 there were some 20 SEZs. In 2005, the number was expanded into the hundreds in a renewed drive to attract manufacturing FDI.

Economic growth

Post-reform India is an interesting case. Fifty per cent of India's GDP comes from services, but the country still has a large agricultural sector and it lacks a major manufacturing base. Compare India with China, where manufacturing dominates. India could be said to have **leapfrogged** towards a service economy, missing out

	Infosys	Wipro	TCS (Tata group)
Founded	1981	1945	1968
Headquarters	Bangalore	Bangalore	Mumbai
Employees	104 000	97 000	143 000
Main areas of operation	Software services	ICT services	Software, business services
Rank in the Forbes Global 2000 list, 2009	891	989	834

Table 6.1
India's leading BPO companies

the industrialisation stage of development. In fact, much of the country is still agricultural with booming services in a few locations. **Outsourcing** has been one of the keys to India's success. Growth has focused on call centres and other back-office administrative work, plus software development. Often a TNC outsources to India, and later 'spins off' the outsourced business so it is run wholly by a local Indian company. The TNC then buys the services it requires but does not have any other overheads. Numerous TNCs have outsourced:

- In the 1980s, British Airways and American Express pioneered the transfer of call centres and administrative functions to New Delhi.
- In the last 10 years there has been a flood of outsourcing involving companies such as Norwich Union (now Aviva), Axa, Accenture, Dell and Lloyds TSB.
- By 2004, several large Indian information technology services companies had emerged. These companies take on the back-office functions for TNCs. Technically this is called business process outsourcing (BPO). They include Infosys and Wipro (see Table 6.1).
- Increasingly, TNCs are locating research and development functions in India. Hewlett-Packard announced in 2009 that it was setting up HP Software Universities in eight Indian cities to train software testers. Honeywell International announced it was investing $50 million in a research and development facility in Bangalore employing 3000 people.

Table 6.2
India's BPO scorecard

Positives	Score		
Wage costs — a skilled ICT, software or call centre worker earns $4000–10 000 per year, much lower than in Europe and even China. Wages are beginning to rise	✓	✓	
Skilled labour — Karnataka State alone has 77 colleges churning out 29 000 graduates each year. In general, education levels are lower than in China, but not at graduate level. Rapid growth has led to some labour shortages in some sectors	✓		
English — widely spoken by graduates and the middle class, and is important for North American and European businesses, especially for call centre outsourcing	✓	✓	✓
Infrastructure — much less well developed than in China, but for service industries which are footloose this is less important than it would be for manufacturing. Power shortages are a growing problem	✗	✗	
Working practices — workers are prepared to work long hours and flexible shifts; union membership is not a well-known concept, as most workers are first generation urbanites	✓	✓	
Red tape — doing business in India is a long, drawn-out process of permit and licence getting; bribes are common. Local BPO companies remove the need for this. India ranked 122nd in the 2009 World Bank ease of doing business rankings.	✗	✗	✗
Political stability — India's democracy is stable, but the country has been a regular target for terrorist attacks particularly in Mumbai, e.g. the attacks on hotels in 2008	✓		

IT, software, BPO and call centres have seen startling growth in the last few years. IT outsourcing in India in 2008 was estimated to employ 700 000 workers and be valued at $11 billion. Annual growth rates have been 30–35% in recent years and India has some 40% of the global market in IT outsourcing. This last figure is significant; what is it about India that has allowed it to become a global player so rapidly? In Table 6.2, India is evaluated as a location for outsourcing.

It is important to recognise that a decision to outsource services and back-office functions to India is not a simple one. It is certainly more complex than just cheap labour. If cheap labour were the only consideration, then TNCs would presumably outsource to sub-Saharan Africa.

Case study 15 — TATA: EMERGING TNC

India's middle class has tripled since the early 1990s and 50% of the population is predicted to be middle class by 2025. About 1% of the poor cross the poverty line each year. The percentage living on less than $1 per day has fallen from 42% in 1995 to 35% in 2008, but the total number remains about the same due to population growth. Poverty is high in India compared with its BRIC competitors.

As Bangalore, Chennai, Pune and other centres for BPO have grown, the burgeoning middle class have created a virtuous cycle by investing their salaries into consumption, further fuelling the growth in services. India's first budget airline, Kingfisher Red, was founded in 2003. This has spawned numerous low-cost competitor airlines such as Spice-Jet, Indigo and GoAir. Around 8 million new mobile phone customers sign up each month.

One company well placed to take advantage of India's new consumers is Tata Group. Tata is a vast industrial conglomerate based in Mumbai (Table 6.3). It ranks about 90th in the list of the world's largest companies — similar in size to Sony or Peugeot–Citroen.

Tata Group has a global strategy which in the last 15 years has led it to a series of high-profile takeovers and acquisitions, propelling it to a position of global significance:
- In 2000, Tetley Tea was bought by Tata Tea.
- In 2007, Tata Steel bought Corus Steel (formerly British Steel) for $12 billion with steel plants on Teeside, at Port Talbot and Scunthorpe.
- In 2008, Tata Motors bought Jaguar Land Rover from Ford for $2 billion.

Table 6.3
Some of the Tata Group companies

Tata is becoming India's leading global brand. Other Indian brands include Arcelor Mittal, which is the world's largest steel company, but beyond that Indian companies are generally not well known. Tata shot to fame in 2008 with the launch of its Nano car.

350,000 employees 96 different companies in Group $60 billion+ sales 2007–08 Operates in 80 countries (60% of sales outside India)				
Tata Motors	**Tata Steel**	**Tata Communications**	**Tata Tea**	**Tata Power**
The world's 19th biggest vehicle maker although expanding rapidly	The world's sixth largest steel maker, producing 20–30 million tonnes per year	India's largest telecommunication provider. It operates the world's largest marine fibre-optic communication network	The world's second largest maker and distributor of tea, employing around 60 000 people	India's largest private power generator with a capacity of about 2700 MW in 2008

Figure 6.2
The Nano car

TopFoto

The Nano is important in a number of ways:

- It is designed to cost 123 000 rupees, or around $2500 and is aimed at India's new middle class.
- It is small, suitable for India's roads, but still has four doors.
- The stated aim of the Nano is to get Indians off their mopeds and into cars.
- The Nano has been designed with a European version, the Europa, for export.
- Everything that could be cut, has been. The Nano has one windscreen wiper, no opening boot, one side mirror and no power steering.

The Nano also illustrates some of the tensions of India's economic progress. The Nano might be said to reflect the poor, low-tech side of India — the side with 34% of the population still living on less than $1 per day. Tata's most expensive car is the Range Rover Sport V8, costing around £64 000 — easily within reach of India's 123 000 millionaires (Merrill Lynch, 2007).

Tata's launch plans for the Nano were derailed by an old-fashioned dispute over land. Tata planned to build the Nano factory in Singur, West Bengal, about 50 km north of Calcutta. This is one of India's poorest regions. However, disputes arose over the land for the factory. Farmers claimed that it had been taken by force with no compensation given. The case eventually went to court, and it was found in favour of Tata. The long-running, sometimes violent dispute, convinced Tata to switch production to a new plant in Gujarat, delaying the car's launch until 2009.

Tata is clearly a global force with aspirations to continue to grow — largely by taking over other companies. In India, Tata alone accounts for some 3% of Indian GDP. The company does face risks. Its reliance on vehicle production, steel and other industrials means it was hit particularly hard by the global downturn in 2008. In some developed countries it would be broken up into smaller, leaner, more focused companies.

Question

(a) India is a difficult country to classify. Is it a least developed country, newly industrialising country (NIC) or developed country? Outline the evidence.
(b) 'TNCs move to India because of cheap labour.' To what extent is this statement true?
(c) Explain why Tata has bought a number of companies in the developed world.

Guidance

(a) You can probably dismiss 'developed country' relatively easily — although some Indian TNCs are 'world class' and its nuclear power and space programme are high-tech. India does have some of the characteristics of a least developed country — for example, its agricultural sector and HDI. It is a country with huge numbers of very poor people. It is industrialising, but not in the 'standard' way as the focus has been on services rather than manufacturing. The truth is probably that it depends where in India you choose to look — Bangalore and rural West Bengal are poles apart in terms of level of development.
(b) Cheap labour is an oversimplification. Try to identify the other factors that have attracted companies, especially in the service sector, to India.
(c) Tata has taken the trend for Western TNCs to invest in Asia, and reversed it. By buying Corus and Jaguar Land Rover it has acquired world-class companies, their brand images and their technology. This is a quick and easy way to expand and build a worldwide image and presence.

Case study 16 — BARRIERS TO INDIAN DEVELOPMENT

India's emerging power status is at a crossroads. It has enjoyed strong economic growth since the 1990s but its neighbour China has done better. The gap between the two nations has widened as India has broken out of the Hindu rate of growth, but not achieved the dragon's rate (Table 6.4).

India remains two nations, the rural poor and the urban rich. The urban rich are concentrated in a few locations that have benefited from India's growing service sector — Mumbai, Delhi, Chennai and Bangalore. As Figure 6.3 shows, wealth in India is concentrated in the south and west of the country around these urban-growth poles. Incomes in large swathes of India average under $1 per day.

India remains a rural country. Only 29% of people live in urban areas compared with 43% in China and over 80% in Brazil. An industrial India would imply mass migration to cities, with all the problems that entails in terms of housing, healthcare, education and sanitation provision. In many ways India's economy is skewed towards this majority rural population. The government subsidises fertilisers and fuel, both of which are needed by farmers. According to *The Economist*, fertiliser subsidies amounted to $26 billion in 2008. Fuel subsidies cost a further $12 billion. This money might be better spent on education and healthcare. Subsidies tend to support inefficient producers who, in a subsidy-free market, would be taken over to improve productivity. India relies on

Table 6.4
Annual % growth of GDP in China and India, 1999–2008

	2008	2007	2006	2005	2004	2003	2002	2001	2000	1999
China	9.8	11.9	10.7	10.4	10.1	10	9.1	8.3	8.4	7.6
India	6.6	9	9.2	9.2	8.3	8.4	3.7	5.2	4	7.4

imports for 75% of its oil. When oil prices spiked in 2008, the fuel subsidy quickly moved from a drain on government resources to a crisis in financing. Cutting fuel and fertiliser subsidies is extremely unpopular.

Infrastructure is India's biggest challenge, and it is a huge one. In 2008, only 13% of Indians were connected to any form of sewage treatment system. Some 700 million do not have access to a connected toilet. This is a potential disease time bomb, especially in rapidly expanding cities. In terms of roads, India compares unfavourably with China, having just 8000 km of dual carriageway compared with China's 50000 km plus. The Indian government does have a plan for roads. The Golden Quadrilateral highway project (Figure 6.4) is a $6 billion plan to link up India's major cities by road. This involves 5000 km of four-lane and six-lane roads. As of 2009, about 90% of the roads were complete — the original date for 100% completion was 2006. India plans to have a 40000 km network of such roads, although this is likely to take decades to complete.

Some resources are potential barriers to India's progress. The most urgent of these is power. No country can develop industrially without reliable supplies of electricity and this India lacks:

- Power cuts, caused by demand outstripping supply are common, sometimes for up to 24 hours.
- Peak electricity demand in 2007 and 2008 was about 15% higher than supply.
- In 2004, the World Bank estimated that 60% of small and medium-sized businesses had their own generators, adding to costs but increasing reliability.
- Sixty per cent of the Indian population have no access to electricity, mostly in rural areas.

India's future power demands are likely to be huge, possibly needing 500000 MW of additional capacity by 2020. In 2007, China managed to add 100000 MW in one year whereas India managed 7000 MW — considered a 'good' year by economists.

Water, too, might derail the Indian dream. The water situation across India is approaching crisis proportions.

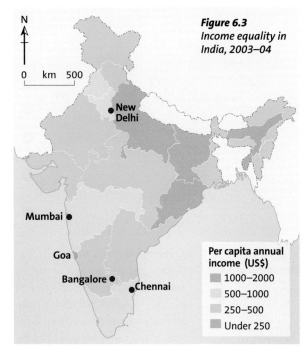

Figure 6.3
Income equality in India, 2003–04

Per capita annual income (US$)
- 1000–2000
- 500–1000
- 250–500
- Under 250

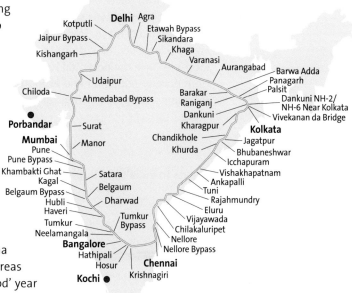

Figure 6.4
The Golden Quadrilateral highway

1. Unresolved dispute over Kashmir, a constant source of tension between India and Pakistan, both now nuclear powers.

2. Taliban and other Muslim extremists from Afghanistan could destabilise Pakistan, which in turn could force India to protect its borders more aggressively.

3. The long-running civil war in Sri Lanka seemed to reach a conclusion in 2009 but only time will tell if it is over for good.

4. Tibet remains a source of tension with the Tibetan leader, the Dalai Lama, resident in India while China controls Tibet.

5. In 2008 Nepal become a communist republic, overturning the rule of its Monarchy. This happened peacefully but Nepal's recent history has been turbulent.

6. Muslim Bangladesh and Hindu India have had tense relations. India fears mass migration from poverty stricken Bangladesh, especially if flooding increases in frequency.

7. Burma and India share a border. Internal conflict against Burma's despotic regime could spill over India's border.

Figure 6.5
Unstable South Asia

A United Nations human development report in 2006 suggested that 25% of New Delhi's population had no access to piped water at all and another 25% had running water for less than 3 hours per day. Buying water from private vendors costs around $20 per month, which is a lot in a country with widespread poverty. Farmers routinely deplete groundwater supplies using illegal wells and pumps powered by government subsidised fuel. Many rivers are polluted by human sewage. The Yamuna River in Delhi is biologically dead, polluted by sewage so much that faecal coliforms are 100 000 times the safe level. Longer term, climate change is likely to reduce water supplies from the Himalaya mountains as glaciers which provide spring and summer meltwater disappear.

Geopolitics could be an issue for India as it occupies a troubled area of the world. The instability of South Asia is partly a hangover from the colonial era and the nightmare of India's partition. Just before independence in 1947, millions of Hindus and Muslims migrated into the two new countries created by partition — India (Hindu) and Pakistan (Muslim). Pakistan was split into West Pakistan (Pakistan as it is today) and East Pakistan, now Bangladesh. The mass migrations were accompanied by violence and death. Figure 6.5 shows the current sources of instability in South Asia. Any of the unstable locations have the potential to flare up, dragging India into conflicts and distracting it from poverty reduction and economic development. Keeping up with the other BRICs represents such a challenge for India that distractions are the last thing the country needs.

15

Using case studies

Question

What are the threats to India's continued status as an emerging power?

Guidance

Consider political, economic, environmental and social threats to give your answer structure. Socially many Indians, particularly those in rural areas, have yet to benefit from India's progress. Could this pose a future threat? India is a fairly stable democracy but political turmoil surrounds its borders and some tensions have the potential to spill over. Most economists agree that infrastructure is a key challenge that India has yet to tackle head-on in the way that China has. Water, transport and energy all have the potential to slow growth to a crawl. Much of India's environmental management infrastructure has the qualities of a poor country, not an 'Asian Tiger'.

Declining superpowers

Is decline inevitable?

Some economic theories suggest that superpowers have a finite life. The most famous is long-wave theory. This theory was pioneered in the 1920s by the Russian economist N. D. Kondratiev. He identified long timescale economic cycles that have become known as Kondratiev waves. Each wave consists of a peak, when economic growth and prosperity is high, and a trough which corresponds to a depression. Each wave is linked to the development and spread of a new suite of technologies (Figure 7.1). This creates demand, sales and trade and, therefore, wealth. Depression sets in when demand is saturated. Growth only resumes when a new suite of technologies and products is developed.

The timing and exact nature of the long waves is disputed, but not the general theory. For geographers, the most interesting aspect of the theory is the changing location of each wave's new innovations. From 1800, the location has shifted from Europe to North America and now towards Asia. It is interesting to speculate that the global downturn of 2007–10 may be the end of the fifth wave. By most measures this recession is the worst since the 1930s, which ended the third wave. Will the

Figure 7.1
Long-wave economic cycles

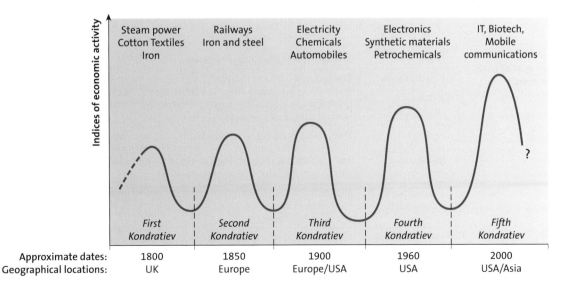

sixth wave belong to Asia and, if so, what type of new innovations and technologies might it be based on? Some emerging technologies may provide clues:

- truly efficient and competitive renewable energy technologies such as thin-film photo-voltaic, or possibly hydrogen transport technology linked to renewable electricity generation
- gene therapy and drugs tailored to fit individuals; for over a decade genetic medicine has made big promises but failed so far to deliver
- nanotechnology, essentially atomic-scale engineering and machines
- artificial intelligence; computers that are so powerful they mimic human brains

With the benefit of hindsight, it seems obvious that the second wave would be based on railways and steel, but it is much less clear looking forward to the sixth wave.

The idea of market saturation is important in explaining the falling limb of a long-wave cycle. In order to break the fall, a new product and new markets have to be found. We have already seen the vast size of the Indian and Chinese markets — 2.5 billion people. Perhaps this makes it inevitable that the next 'boom' will be Asian.

The unknown

'There are known knowns. There are things we know we know. There are known unknowns. That is to say, we know there are some things we do not know. But there are also unknown unknowns, the ones we don't know we don't know.'

If you can unpick this quote you may, one day, be Defense Secretary of the USA. This quote was made by Donald Rumsfeld in 2002. He was both lampooned and praised for his quote. The basic idea of an 'unknown unknown' is that there are some events that are genuinely surprising and cannot be planned for. Such events have been called 'black swan events' by the academic Nassim Taleb. The term relates to the discovery of black swans in Australia in the eighteenth century by European explorers who had assumed that all swans were white because the only swans they had ever seen until then were white. Taleb states that black swan events are large, have a major impact, but are a total surprise (see Table 7.1). Due to the surprise nature

Table 7.1
The impact of black swan events

Event	Impact on geopolitics and superpowers
First World War	The nature, length and carnage of the First World War were unexpected. It ended the global hegemony of the British Empire and ushered the USA onto the world stage as a global power. The 1920s and 1930s were two decades without dominant superpowers
Post Second World War UK bankruptcy	The Second World War was expected, but the bankruptcy of the UK and the need for US loans were not. The rapid collapse of the British Empire between 1945 and 1960 was mostly because the UK could no longer afford an empire and as such it ceased to be a superpower
The collapse of communism	The USSR and eastern Europe looked shaky in the 1980s but no one predicted total collapse between 1989 and 1990. The post-Cold War world left the USA as the only superpower
The 9/11 attacks in the USA	Terrorism could be predicted, but not on this scale. The reaction of the USA (the invasion of Iraq, the global war on terror) has arguably weakened the power of the US ideology

of the event they have the potential to cause major shifts in economics and politics because reactions to them cannot be planned in advance.

While Kondratiev's long waves work in the background, Taleb's black swans are the events on the front pages. Perhaps a combination of inevitable long-term changes and opportunities and challenges created by one-off events is what determines who the superpowers are.

Ageing superpowers

One uncomfortable 'known known' is the issue of ageing. In some developed nations it is already a political and geographical issue. Ageing, or greying, creates a large dependent population that has to be supported by the working-age population. Total fertility rate, the average number of children born to each woman, gives us a good indication of future population (Table 7.2).

Very low		Close to replacement		Moderate	
South Korea	1.21	UK	1.82	Kuwait	2.18
Spain	1.41	China	1.73	Brazil	2.25
Italy	1.38	France	1.89	Bahrain	2.29
Japan	1.27	USA	2.05	UAE	2.31
Russia	1.34			Qatar	2.66
Germany	1.36			India	2.81

Table 7.2
Total fertility rates 2005–10 (United Nations)

Countries in the very low category in Table 7.2 face declining populations and rapid greying, unless they can use immigration to boost the population. Some countries, for example Japan and South Korea, have never been positive towards large-scale immigration. The BRICs are spread across the spectrum of fertility rates, but the USA has higher fertility than both China and Russia. This reflects larger US families plus the impact of immigration. Immigrants tend to be young and often come from locations with a culture of larger families. Ageing is important because it brings with it significant costs:

- In Japan in 2025, there will be 2.5 working people to support each pensioner and the costs of social security payments to the elderly is expected to have grown from 90 trillion yen to 140 trillion yen.
- Taxes may have to rise to pay for pensions, healthcare and retirement homes. This is money that could have been invested in education or infrastructure.
- Shortages of skilled workers will arise. This will increase labour costs and reduce competitiveness. Immigration could plug skills gaps, but it has social costs.
- A youthful workforce is seen as entrepreneurial and innovative whereas an ageing workforce has experience, but lacks dynamism.

What countries fear most is a downward ageing spiral with rising benefits and pensions costs, but no young workers because fertility continues to decline. This is a serious worry for some European and Asian countries, including China. The USA seems so far to have avoided this problem.

Question

(a) Explain Kondratiev's long-wave theory.

(b) Why might different countries (superpowers and emerging powers) have very different feelings about Kondratiev's waves?

(c) Which countries have the most to fear from an ageing population?

Guidance

(a) Examine Figure 7.1 carefully and ensure that you comment on the timing of the waves, the technologies of the waves and the changing geographical locations.

(b) The emerging superpowers may view the waves (specifically the next wave) as their chance to move to the prime position in terms of economic power. The EU and USA might see diminished power as the economic nexus shifts away from them. The energy giants in the Gulf and Russia would probably see increased sales on the horizon.

(c) Ageing is a mixed picture. It is not as simple as the BRICs versus the 'old' powers because China and Russia have ageing populations but the USA has a relatively youthful one. Japan and some EU countries have much to fear, as their ageing situations may approach crisis levels sooner rather than later.

Case study **17** THE COLLAPSE OF COMMUNISM

The 1988 Olympics in Seoul, South Korea, passed off with predictable results. The USSR topped the medals table, its East German ally was second and the USA trailed in third place. Four years later, in Barcelona, there was no USSR or East German team. Both countries had ceased to exist and the Cold War was over. What had happened? The communist system in the USSR and eastern Europe was based on a political and economic ideology:

- government ownership and control of industry and employment
- full employment and a government-run education, health and social welfare system
- a rejection of private ownership of property, for example housing and businesses
- a powerful one-party state, with no free elections or free press

Communism is based on the ideas of Karl Marx. It aims to create an egalitarian society. The foundation stone of Marxism is to reject the private ownership of business — what Marx called the 'means of production'. Marx argued that the owners of business, the bourgeoisie, will always seek to exploit workers (the proletariat) to maximise their own profits. For ordinary people, this means low wages and poor working conditions. While the USSR and eastern Europe never achieved Marx's ideal they did reject capitalism and private enterprise. Communist countries had some successes. Education standards, healthcare and the involvement of women in the workforce generally matched or bettered standards in the 'West'. Lack of freedom, low per capita incomes and shortages of goods were sources of tension. Figure 7.2 shows how communism was swept from Europe in 1989–90.

The collapse, rather like a domino effect, critically undermined the USSR. In February 1990, the communist party in the USSR gave up its monopoly on power, ending the dream of a socialist state which began with the 1917 Russian revolution. In the space

Figure 7.2
The collapse of communism in eastern Europe

The union Solidarity is allowed to participate in Polish elections ending Communist Party rule, September 1989

EAST GERMANY

The 'Iron Curtain'

USSR

East Germans begin migrating west through Hungary's open border with Austria. The Berlin Wall falls, November 1989

POLAND

CZECHOSLOVAKIA

HUNGARY

Non-violent 'Velvet revolution' overthrows Communist Party in Czechoslovakia, November 1989

ROMANIA

BULGARIA

Hungarian parliament votes to establish a multi-party democracy, October 1989

Communist Party in Bulgaria gives up power, early 1990

Brief but violent clashes remove the Communist leaders of Romania, December 1989

of 2 years, the world moved from the bipolar Cold War world to a unipolar world, with the USA as the unchallenged superpower. What caused communism to collapse?

- Economic stagnation occurred in the 1980s. Incomes remained flat and people began to wonder if communism was bringing them any benefits.
- There was discontent over the USSR's invasion of Afghanistan, which was seen by many ordinary people in the USSR as a pointless conflict, yet one that cost 15 000 Soviet lives.
- In order to try and reduce discontent the USSR's leader, Mikhail Gorbachev, introduced a series of reforms. *Perestroika* increased political freedom and *glasnost* increased economic freedom. These reforms had the effect of undermining the whole communist system because criticism of the leadership was possible.
- The Chernobyl nuclear disaster in 1986 undermined people's faith in Soviet technology. Initially, the state tried to cover up the disaster.
- Satellite television and global news channels began to allow people in communist countries access to 'Western' information.
- Rising crime, alcoholism and drug use made the system look corrupting and suggested that the state could not solve all problems.

Following the collapse, the republics that had formed the USSR (e.g. Latvia, Georgia and Kazakhstan) quickly declared their independence, leaving Russia as a separate country. The lesson from the collapse of communism is that economic growth is important to maintain stability, as is the support of the majority of people. When people begin to question the ability of a superpower to create prosperity and solve everyday problems then its time is probably drawing to a close.

Credit crunch

A valid question is whether the 'credit crunch' or global financial crisis/recession that began in 2008 qualifies as a black swan event. To say the crisis was unexpected is not quite true. In 2006, Nouriel Roubini, an economics professor at New York University, predicted just such financial and economic meltdown. In 2006 Roubini was seen as being a little mad; by late 2007, he was being hailed as a prophet. The credit crunch might be better described as a 'known unknown' — we knew it would happen, but not when.

The crisis was caused by the following:

- There had been risky 'sub-prime' mortgage lending in the USA. When the US housing market and economy began to slow, defaults on these mortgages rose leaving banks with bad debts.
- Many banks had also lent money to businesses and investors. These loans were often high risk, so the smallest economic downturn turned them sour.
- With hindsight, the oil price, which reached the unprecedented level of $147 per barrel in 2008, combined with very high food prices, may have been a major reason for the slowdown that turned into a tsunami of bad debt.

Figure 7.3
The geography of the credit crunch (inset graph is the AIG commodity price index)

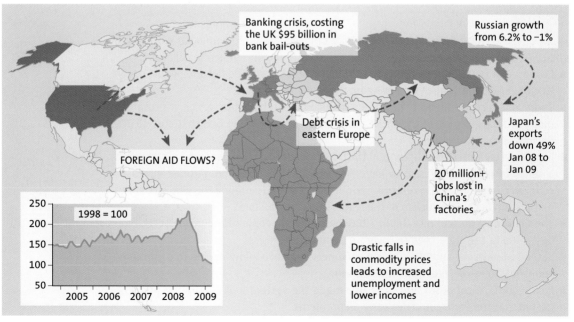

Banking crisis, costing the UK $95 billion in bank bail-outs

Russian growth from 6.2% to −1%

Debt crisis in eastern Europe

Japan's exports down 49% Jan 08 to Jan 09

FOREIGN AID FLOWS?

20 million+ jobs lost in China's factories

1998 = 100

Drastic falls in commodity prices leads to increased unemployment and lower incomes

The credit crunch illustrates the inter dependence of a globalised world. The wave of economic turmoil that swept the world in 2008–09 is shown in Figure 7.3.

The outcome of the credit crunch has been a recession (6 months or more of negative economic growth) and rising unemployment. In the developed world, the mountain of bank debt has been transformed by bank bail-outs and buy-outs into a mountain of government debt:

■ In the USA by June 2009, the government had guaranteed banks, or bailed them out to prevent collapse, to the tune of some $8.5 trillion.
■ In the UK, the government guarantee and spending on bail-outs amounted to $1.2 trillion.
■ Stimulus packages to boost economies totalled $940 billion in the USA, $30 billion in the UK, $100 billion in Germany and $590 billion in China.

Most of this money is debt and will have to be paid back. The worry for the EU and USA superpowers is that the debts are now so large that they will take decades to pay back. In the meantime, the BRICs, led by China, will power ahead and gain ground. Unfortunately, Japan's recent history suggests that this scenario is possible.

Lessons from Japan

In the 1980s, Japan was talked of as the next superpower. The country had undergone an 'economic miracle' from the 1960s when its economy had rapidly industrialised. Figure 7.4 shows how per capita GDP caught and passed that of the UK and USA in the 20 years from 1960 to 1980. By the mid 1980s, Japan was exporting its success, opening a succession of car 'transplants' abroad — for example, Nissan in Sunderland and Toyota in Derby. Between 1981 and 1991, Honda, Toyota, Nissan and Mazda opened 14 transplants in the USA and Canada with a capacity to build over 3 million vehicles per year.

Seemingly powering ahead, fuelled by investment around the world, per capita GDP pushed way beyond US levels only to hit a wall in 1991 and remain stagnant for over a decade (referred to as 'the lost decade' in Japan). What happened to cause this abrupt reversal of fortunes?

■ First, a credit bubble was created by speculative investment and property development. This pushed property prices to unsustainable levels.

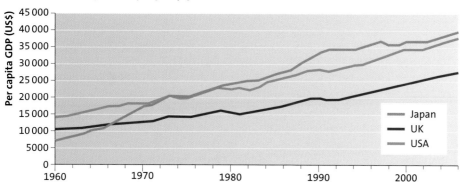

Figure 7.4
Per capita GDP growth in the UK, USA and Japan, 1960–2006

- Second, the Bank of Japan increased interest rates to make borrowing money more expensive and dampen down the property bubble. This led to a collapse in property values and a decline in the value of the Nikkei stock market index from a peak of 35000 in 1989 to 17000 3 years later. With property and stock values collapsing, a debt crisis began.
- Third, the Bank of Japan kept interest rates at 4–6% from 1990 to 1992, which encouraged saving not spending. This eventually led to deflation (falling prices) and even less incentive to spend. The net result was sharply falling consumption and a stagnant economy.

During the 1990s, Japan's chance to become an economic superpower slipped away as its economy grew by only 0–1% per year while that of the rest of the developed world grew at 2–3%, and China and India powered ahead at 8–10% growth. It might have been expected that a few years after the 1989–90 collapse Japan would recover, but it did not. The reasons for this include:
- Japanese consumers resumed their traditional frugal lifestyle, and did not return to high-end fashion and consuming imported whisky.
- Japan's ageing population is naturally conservative and few families are being created that might fuel the sales of consumer goods.
- Some argue that the innovative, high-tech, youthful thrust has gone from Japan because in 2008 the average age in Japan was 44 years, compared with 37 in the USA and 34 in China.
- In some countries, immigration is used to create a youthful, enterprising culture. Japan has one of the lowest rates of immigration in the world; as a nation it is respectful of foreigners but they are not encouraged to make Japan their home.

Japan's story is, in many ways, a tale of lost opportunities. Just as it seemed to be breaking into the big league, the bubble burst. Many economists argue that Japan's government acted too late, and did too little, to prevent an economic crisis turning into a decade of stagnation and relative decline.

17 Using case studies

Question

(a) How unusual was the collapse of the USSR and Warsaw Pact? Compare its collapse to the end of other superpowers.

(b) 'Almost made it.' How far is this statement true of Japan's aspirations to be an economic superpower?

Guidance

(a) The USSR collapsed very rapidly. Even with the benefit of hindsight, the collapse looks precipitous. You should consider that there was no great external shock, war or violent internal uprising. Communist eastern Europe and the USSR moved from a position of power to collapse in a handful of years. The decline of the British Empire was spread over 20 or more years and included one, if not two, world wars.

(b) The statement fits the economic position of Japan well, as the beginning of the lost decade ended Japan's chances of challenging the USA. However, remember that being a superpower means more than simply economic wealth — consider if Japan's military, culture and global politics were up to superpower standards.

THE USA: HYPERPOWER OR HAS-BEEN?

Japan and the USSR may have lessons for the USA as it confronts the rise of the BRICs, especially China. The USA has some trump cards. Its technological and military strength are not under threat and it has a youthful population. Ideologically, the USA has a relatively homogeneous population with the vast majority of people believing firmly in capitalism, and economic and personal freedom. It is beginning to lose ground economically. Table 7.3 shows the changing numbers of the world's 500 largest TNCs, located in selected countries. The decline of the USA and the rise of China, even in this short period, are obvious. These figures partly pre-date the 'credit crunch' and suggest that China is beginning to compete globally with the USA.

The USA has recognised that its time as a hyperpower may be drawing to a close. The US government Department for National Intelligence (DNI) released a report in 2008 entitled *Global Trends 2025: A Transformed World*. This report recognises a number of key trends, which are outlined in Table 7.4.

A likely scenario is that the economic power of China will rise, gradually, to meet that of the USA. This is very different to the USSR's collapse and the stagnation of Japan. If this does happen, the world could end up with two large superpower spheres of influence, in the Americas (USA) and east Asia (China), and several smaller ones for instance in Europe, south Asia and central Asia. Precipitous US decline in the face of the rising BRICs is unlikely for a number of reasons:

■ Despite China's advances, the USA's TNCs remain strong and these, particularly retail and media companies, help project its global image and aspirations.

Fortune global 500: companies by country	2005	2006	2007	2008	Change 2005–08
USA	176	170	162	153	−23
Japan	81	70	67	64	−17
France, Germany and UK	111	111	108	110	−1
China	16	20	24	29	+13
India	5	6	6	7	+2
Russia	3	5	4	5	+2
Brazil	3	4	5	5	+2

Table 7.3
Top 500 TNCs by country, 2005–08 (Fortune magazine)

Table 7.4
Trends identified by the DNI, 2008

Key trend	Possible impact on the USA
A multipolar world system is emerging with the rise of China, India and others. The unprecedented shift in wealth and power from West to East will continue	USA continues to have influence in Europe and Latin America but influence declines in Asia–Pacific region and possibly in Africa
USA remains the single most powerful country in 2025, but is less dominant	Continued high defence spending; difficult choice — to remain the 'global policeman' or withdraw
Economic growth and 1.2 billion more people by 2025 increases pressure on energy, food and water resources	Increased wealth possibly offset by high oil and food prices. New areas of tension over water and land
Growing young, male, disenchanted populations who are underemployed represent a serious risk in the Near East and Middle East. Terrorism is unlikely to disappear by 2025, but it may reduce if economic growth continues and people become more satisfied	Continued need to be involved politically and militarily in the Middle East, and therefore high military costs and political difficulties at home, i.e. justifying involvement to the public

- The USA is a powerful force for innovation and technological advancement. In terms of new patents, it is second only to Japan and in terms of royalties it leads the world, taking 41% of all global royalty and licence fees in 2008.
- Despite the economic crisis that began in 2008, the USA has strong economic growth potential — for instance, it does not face the ageing crisis that Europe faces.

Nevertheless, the USA needs to solve a number of key issues that threaten its hegemony:
- Energy security is important, especially in a country that is running out of its own oil. Diversifying its energy resources and cutting oil imports is one reason that the USA has moved rapidly into Brazilian-style biofuels.
- Rogue and failed states, plus terrorist groups, could derail the USA forcing it into a long-term conflict of attrition similar to the Vietnam War of the 1960s and 1970s. This war showed that the USA could become a divided nation. A significant US fear is that nuclear weapons fall into the hands of a terrorist organisation of a rogue state which could effectively hold the world to ransom.

The day-one challenge facing President Obama when he took office on 20 January 2009 was to stabilise the US economy and prevent the collapse of the US banking system. In 2008 and 2009, the USA took quite extraordinary steps to shore up its faltering economy:
- There was a $1 trillion stimulus package, designed to pump money into the economy and prevent deflation. This is when real prices fall, so people put off spending because goods will be cheaper in the future. This is what drove the Japanese economy downward in the 1990s.
- Banks and other businesses, for example AIG, Citigroup, JP Morgan, GM and Chrysler, were saved with government money. This is effectively nationalisation (government ownership of businesses) and is viewed by many in the USA as anti-capitalist and even anti-American.
- The debts of troubled banks and mortgage lenders were guaranteed to prevent them collapsing. In effect, the debts of private companies were nationalised.

Some estimates suggested that by summer 2009, these actions added up to $6 trillion in government spending and liabilities — 43% of the USA's total GDP. It is clear that the USA is prepared to take unique and unpalatable measures to maintain its position in the world.

Detroit's big three

Nothing illustrates more clearly the difficulties faced by the USA than the decline in its once world-beating car industry. As Figure 7.5 shows, even in 1990 the 'Detroit three' of Chrysler, General Motors and Ford commanded over 70% of US car sales. By 2008, this figure had fallen to below 50%. Ford faced a financial loss of $14.9 billion and GM and Chrysler were both bankrupt, supported only by government funds. American cars were once the envy of the world (Figure 7.6) — large, comfortable and leaders in styling.

The crisis in the US automobile industry has been long in the making. It reflects a poor choice of strategy from Detroit versus a successful one from Japanese competitors.

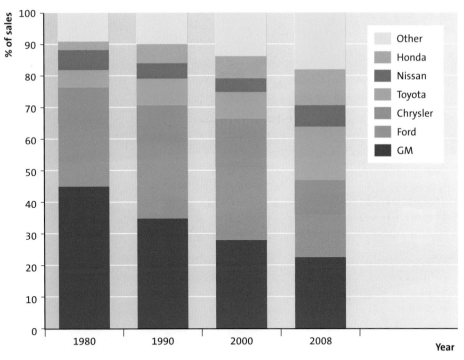

The two strategies are outlined in Table 7.5.

The Detroit 'big three' crisis came to a head in 2009:

- Ford avoided taking US government money but has drastically cut production and is re-tooling SUV and light truck factories to make 'European' small cars such as the Focus and Fiesta to sell in the USA.

GM, Ford and Chrysler	Honda, Nissan and Toyota
Most factories are in Michigan, especially in and around Detroit. These factories lost over 80 000 jobs, 1993–2008	The companies' US factories are in Tennessee, Alabama, Kentucky and the Carolinas. They gained over 90 000 jobs, 1993–2008
Brands which relied on past glories, especially the cars of the 1950s and 60s; gradually brands lost market share and have been ditched e.g. Pontiac, Oldsmobile and Plymouth	Badging cars just for the US market, so they seemed more American, e.g. Infiniti (Nissan), Acura (Honda) and Lexus (Toyota)
Relying on old Detroit factories, workers and expensive union retirement and benefit packages; by 2005, pensions costs were adding $1500–2000 to the price tag of every Detroit car	Building transplant factories in the USA, so Japanese brand cars are made by US workers overcame resistance to 'foreign' cars; new factories avoided the expensive Detroit pay and conditions demanded by the United Autoworkers Union
Focusing on large, big engine V6 and V8 cars; since 2000, Detroit has focused on SUVs and light trucks as these are not subject to government fuel-efficiency rules; when petrol reached $4 per gallon in 2008, sales of these vehicles collapsed	Transplant Japanese cars are much more fuel efficient and of higher quality; Lexus topped the JD Power customer satisfaction survey in the USA for 14 years in a row up to 2008
Detroit has focused on the American market and not exported its cars in large volumes; this over-reliance on one market made it vulnerable	Most Japanese cars sold in the USA are based on models the companies sell worldwide

Table 7.5
Contrasting strategies in the US car industry

Figure 7.6
A 1957 Ford Country station wagon

Anthony Thompson

- Chrysler was supported by the US government and was eventually taken over by the Italian manufacturer Fiat, after bankruptcy restructured its debts.
- GM entered bankruptcy following months of government bail-outs. GM was once the world's largest industrial conglomerate and its brands — Cadillac, Chevrolet, Buick and Pontiac — symbolised the American dream of freedom and mobility.

18 Using case studies

Question

(a) Is the USA likely to inhabit a unipolar, bipolar or multipolar world in the future?

(b) How relevant is the experience of Detroit to the USA as a whole?

Guidance

(a) Examine Case Study 18 carefully and identify economic and political trends. Consider whether the BRICs are likely to challenge the USA in the near future. You should also consider which BRICs are capable of mounting a challenge — just China or others? Remember that the USA would need to lose power, as well as other nations gaining it, for it to be equalled or surpassed.

(b) It would be relatively easy to use Detroit as a metaphor for the whole of the USA. However, the car industry is just one economic sector and the USA is not particularly reliant on manufacturing. In terms of services, finance and high-tech research and development the USA still outperforms virtually all countries. Do not read too much into Detroit's woes. In some ways, Japanese transplants have been remarkably successful in the USA, again suggesting that Detroit has its own specific problems.

Some 3 million people in the USA are employed in the car industry, including factory workers, part suppliers and car dealers. Many of these people will lose their jobs as the companies are forced to shrink their businesses to a size that matches more closely demand for their products. The continued shrinkage of the economic base of Detroit has serious implications. Already the city's population has fallen from 2 million in the 1960s to under 1 million today. The city council is effectively bankrupt and huge areas of central Detroit are given over to abandoned properties and boarded-up businesses. Unemployment in the city had risen to over 20% by May 2009 and 30% of residents received government food stamps. In a city of 900 000 people only four Starbucks remained open. There were 66 Starbucks in San Francisco in May 2009, a city with a population of 800 000.

Superpowers and the environment

ECOLOGICAL FOOTPRINTS

An ecological footprint is the area of productive land needed to provide the resources (food, water, energy, waste disposal) to support an individual for a year. Ecological footprints are measured in global hectares. There are many 'footprint calculators' on the internet. These can be used to calculate individual footprints and are a good way to understand the concept in more depth. The variation in footprints around the world is huge, as is illustrated by Figure 8.1.

In 2005, the biocapacity of the Earth (Figure 8.1) was 2.1 global hectares per person. This can be thought of as the sustainable level of resource use for the planet with its current population. The EU and USA superpowers significantly exceed this level of consumption, as do Russia and Brazil. The Gulf states, illustrated by the United Arab Emirates below, also have large ecological footprints (8.9 global hectares per person in Kuwait and 4.5 in Saudi Arabia). In 2005, China was at the **biocapacity** level per person and India was significantly below it. Examining the components of ecological footprints reveals some important differences:

Figure 8.1
Ecological footprints, 2005

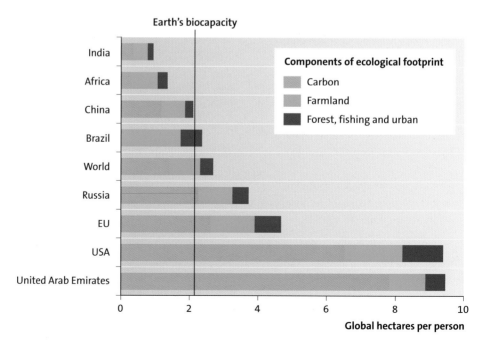

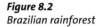
Figure 8.2
Brazilian rainforest

- Brazil's carbon footprint is low because its vast rainforests (Figure 8.2) are a carbon sink and its extensive use of biofuels offsets carbon emissions. Brazil's biofuel experience is seen increasingly as a model for carbon reduction by other nations.
- The UAE has a very large carbon footprint, as do other oil- and gas-rich nations. They tend to be wasteful in terms of fossil fuel consumption as fossil fuels are often subsidised.
- Africa has a low carbon footprint due to lack of cars and electricity, but forests make up a large proportion of its footprint because people tend to rely on fuelwood and wood as a building material.

The superpowers and many of the BRICs are living beyond their means, at least in terms of their impact on the ecology and health of the planet. According to the WWF's *Living Planet Report* (2008) the world as a whole exceeded the Earth's biocapacity as long ago as 1985. By 2040, at the current rates of growth of resource consumption, we will need two planet earths to support our resource consumption. Much of the increased demand will come from India and China.

Future resource demands

Superpowers are very large consumers of resources and because most of these resources are non-renewable, they are also the largest polluters. Figure 8.3 illustrates this, showing that the EU, USA, Japan and BRICs accounted for over 70% of carbon dioxide emissions in 2004.

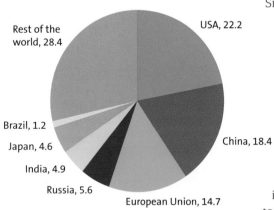

Figure 8.3
Carbon dioxide emisssions in 2004

Since 2004, it is thought China has exceeded the USA's emissions. 'Blame' for rapidly running down oil and gas reserves and polluting the atmosphere falls on these countries, which, in 2004, represented 56% of the world's population.

As the BRICs have gained economic strength in the last decade so demand for resources has risen. There are serious question marks over whether this demand can be met. Most resources we use, including land and energy resources, are finite. With a rising world population and rising incomes in emerging powers such as China, resource consumption is set to rise. Oil has been a source of much attention since prices began rising in 2005. These peaked in August 2008 at $147 per barrel, a record. The *average* price per barrel in 2008 was $100 whereas the average for the entire period from 1976 to 2004 was $23, with a peak of $41 and a low of $12. There are growing concerns that the supply of oil cannot meet demand — this is what is causing high oil prices. Figure 8.4 shows that, since 2004, oil supply has been basically static — what some geologists refer to as 'plateau' oil, i.e. an inability to produce any more oil with current infrastructure. World economic growth between 2004 and 2008 was quite strong at around 3–4% per year, but oil supply did not grow.

Figure 8.4
Oil production, millions of tonnes per year

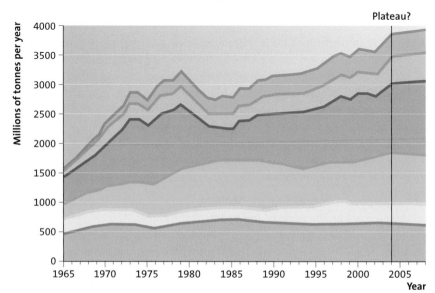

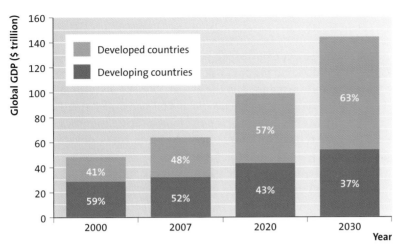

Figure 8.5
Changing global GDP

The economic crisis and subsequent recession that began in 2008 reduced demand for oil, and to some extent oil prices, but the fear is that when the world economy recovers and the BRICs begin to grow rapidly once more, a plateau of oil production will be reached and prices will shoot upward. Longer term, there are question marks over oil supply. Let us assume that over the next 15 years per capita GDP in the BRICs doubles. For India, this would only mean incomes rising from $2500 to $5000. If oil consumption also doubled the world would need to provide the BRICs with an additional 800 million barrels of oil per day. More oil would be needed if other countries also grew.

Of course, there are alternatives. Energy could be supplied in other forms, such as wind, solar, biomass and other renewables, so that oil supplies did not have to rise. It is not only oil that the BRICS need. They have large demands for timber, metal ores, minerals and food. One key issue is the nutrition transition that accompanies development. Increasing numbers of Chinese, Indians and Brazilians are moving towards a protein-rich diet of meat and fish and away from a diet dominated by 'poor' carbohydrates, i.e. rice, wheat and maize. Meat and fish represent a middle-class aspirational diet, but unfortunately these are energy intensive foods. Figure 8.5 shows one possible scenario for future global GDP growth to 2030. Notice that the share of global GDP taken by the developed countries (EU, USA, Japan and others) versus the developing world is projected to reverse. GDP is broadly projected to triple by 2030 which might imply a tripling of resource consumption. Is this even possible on a planet that seems to be using most of its resources already?

Another way of examining the resource problem is to consider the implications of China growing into a superpower broadly as wealthy per person as the USA is today. On current trends this could happen around 2040, and would mean:

■ around 1 billion cars in China, more than the world total of 800 million today
■ 1350 million tonnes of grain consumed per year, or 66% of 2007 world production
■ 180 million tonnes of meat consumed per year, or 80% of 2007 world production
■ 2.8 billion tonnes coal burnt each year, compared to current global production of 2.6 billion tonnes

These levels of consumption are just for China, so global levels, assuming income rises in India, Brazil, Russia, the USA and EU, would be much higher.

What should a superpower or emerging power do if it needs to raise food production but lacks the land to do so? In the past, colonies were the answer but today more subtle ways of acquiring land are required. In the period 2006–09 up to 20 million hectares of foreign farmland was bought by China, India and oil-rich Gulf states (Figure 8.6). Much of the land is in the world's poorest and most food insecure countries. In general, land deals are done government to government. In some cases private companies are involved, often leasing land to grow biofuels.

Some of the land deals are extremely large. It is estimated that 1.5 million hectares of Sudan and close to 3 million hectares in the Democratic Republic of Congo have been leased or sold to foreign buyers. Food grown on the land is shipped back to the investor country. According to the Washington DC based International Food Policy Research Institute the area of land involved in deals since 2006 is equal in size to all of the farmland in France. Certain countries have a strong interest in owning foreign land:

■ Land provides a buffer against rising food prices, such as the doubling of wheat and rice prices in 2006–07.
■ It may be cheaper to grow on foreign land. Farmland in the Middle East is often irrigated at huge expense; foreign land reduces cost.
■ Labour may be cheaper in a foreign country.
■ Land in the home country may be in short supply, meaning reduced food security.

There are difficulties with foreign land policies. First, the strategy smacks of yet another form of neocolonialism, whereby a powerful nation controls aspects of a weaker country. Perhaps more fundamental is the fact that land might be better used to feed the local populations, rather than food being exported to countries that are rich enough to buy food on international markets. The Food and Agriculture Organization's annual publication *The State of Food Insecurity* for 2008 suggested that the proportion of

Figure 8.6
Buying foreign fields in 2009

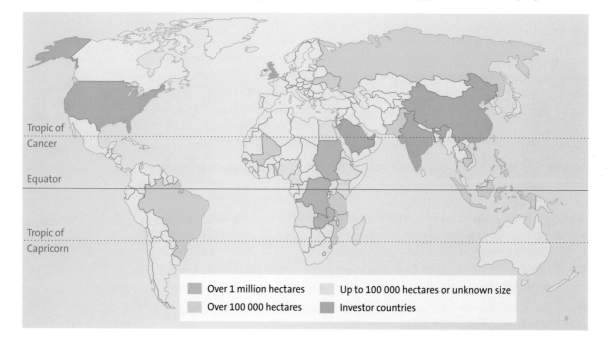

Over 1 million hectares   Up to 100 000 hectares or unknown size

Over 100 000 hectares   Investor countries

undernourished people was 76% in the Democratic Republic of Congo, 21% in Sudan and 45% in Zambia. These three countries are the very ones involved in signing away the largest areas of land to foreign ownership or control.

To some degree signing these deals is understandable. Developing countries often have large areas of land they lack the money and technology to use. Cash in the bank for selling or leasing the land is better than nothing. It is sensible, surely, to question the behaviour of the superpowers and emerging powers in signing these deals. Will they continue to import food or biofuels if one of the developing countries happened to slide towards food crisis and famine?

Using case studies

19 Question

(a) **What is an ecological footprint?**

(b) **Are superpower and emerging power resource consumption levels environmentally sustainable now and will they be sustainable in the future?**

(c) **Summarise the costs and benefits of the 'global land-grab' for both the host and investor countries.**

Guidance

(a) Use Figure 8.1 and the linked text to define a footprint and its components.

(b) The answer to both parts of the question is no. Current levels of consumption seem to be producing excessive pollution and global warming, and are higher than ever before. According to the WWF, the Earth's biocapacity has been exceeded. Future projections of resource consumption are scary. There is little evidence so far that countries are moving towards a more sustainable model.

(c) Consider using a table format to produce your summary:

	Host country	Investor country
Social	+/–	+/–
Economic	+/–	+/–
Environmental	+/–	+/–

THE ARCTIC AND ANTARCTICA

Case study **21**

This chapter has shown how superpowers and emerging powers are likely to place increasing demands on resources in the future. Case Study 14 examined how China's insatiable demand for resources has led it to look to Africa as a source of commodities. Two geographical areas are worth examining in more detail, as they are places where superpowers and emerging power relationships reveal much about contemporary global issues and future trends. The areas are the polar extremes — Antarctica and the Arctic. These two isolated, extreme wildernesses are opposites in many ways. The Antarctic is an isolated continent, mostly of ice-sheet covered land. The Arctic is a polar sea almost entirely surrounded by land masses.

Antarctica shows what the world can do when it works together. In 1959, the Antarctic Treaty set up a unique system of management for the Antarctic continent and the ocean below latitude 60° south:

- Territorial claims were put on hold (see Figure 8.7) and Antarctica was set aside as an area for scientific research.
- Military personnel and all weapons were banned so that the areas became the sole preserve of civilian scientists.
- Various agreements to protect ecosystems and physical systems from exploitation were set up, including a ban on resource exploitation.

Over the decades, 47 countries have signed the Antarctic Treaty, including the USA and USSR (Russia) at the height of the Cold War — a remarkable achievement in many ways. Neither the USA nor Russia has ever claimed Antarctic territory, although both keep permanently manned scientific bases there. The USA Amundsen–Scott base, recently rebuilt at a cost of $150 million, sits right at the South Pole at the intersection of all other Antarctic territorial claims! Figure 8.7 shows the suspected mineral wealth in Antarctica. There are growing fears that as oil and minerals become increasingly scarce, pressure will grow to exploit the resources of the world's last great wilderness.

At the other end of the Earth, this scenario already seems to be playing out. In 2009, the United States Geological Survey (USGS) estimated that 30% of the world's undiscovered natural gas reserves and 13% of oil reserves are within the Arctic. This could mean 90–100 billion barrels of oil. There is no 'Arctic Treaty', but there are territorial disputes as shown in Figure 8.8. These may become increasingly important as more evidence suggests the area is ripe for oil and gas exploitation.

Worryingly, the Arctic lies north of three nuclear powers: the EU, USA and Russia. Increased activity in the area has already resulted in:
- renewed claims by Canada, Norway, Russia and Denmark (which runs Greenland) to extend their 200-mile coastal territorial water zone further into the Arctic Ocean

Figure 8.7
Territorial claims and possible mineral wealth in Antarctica

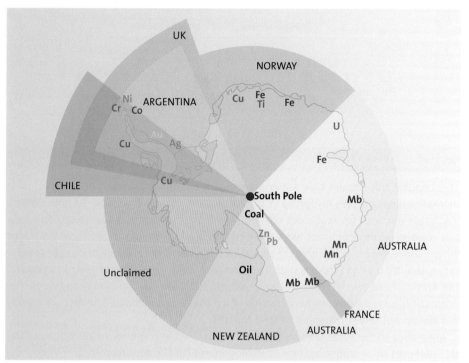

Cu	Copper
Fe	Iron ore
Ti	Titanium
U	Uranium
Mb	Molybdenum
Mn	Manganese
Pb	Lead
Zn	Zinc
Cr	Chromium
Ni	Nickel
Co	Cobalt
Au	Gold
Ag	Silver

Contemporary Case Studies

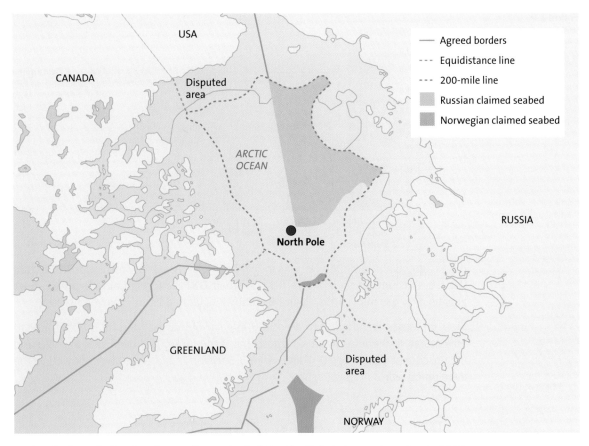

the placing of a Russian flag on the seabed at the North Pole by a submarine in 2007, prompting the Canadian Foreign Minister to remark: 'You can't go around the world these days dropping flags somewhere. This isn't the fourteenth or fifteenth century.'
- scientific teams from Denmark heading for the North Pole in 2007
- Russia announcing in 2009 that it was creating an 'Arctic Force' to protect its Arctic interests

Figure 8.8
The disputed Arctic (all locations approximate)

The Arctic is likely to hot up in more ways than one. Global warming is already making the region easier to access as the sea ice retreats. The more this happens, the easier oil and gas exploitation become. Political tensions will rise as countries seek to make firm claims on the Arctic Ocean. It is the United Nations that will ultimately decide on territorial claims, but any decision will create winners and losers.

Global responsibilities

As has been discussed, superpowers play a key role in international decision making, which brings with it both rights and responsibilities. Many would argue that foreign land-grabs are examples of not respecting rights and of behaving irresponsibly. Many developing countries are wary of superpowers on the basis that they make promises they cannot keep. The most famous of these is an international aid target.

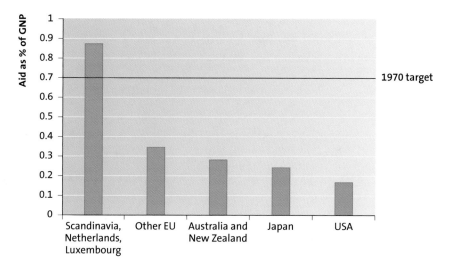

Figure 8.9
Aid from OECD countries in 2006 as a percentage of GNP

It was agreed at the United Nations in 1970 (General Assembly resolution 2626) that the OECD countries should give 0.7% of their GNP as foreign aid. This was to be achieved by the mid 1970s. Figure 8.9 shows what had been achieved by 2006.

Most countries have failed to meet the 40-year-old target, despite it being repeatedly restated. Some estimates suggest that if the target had been met in 1970 and in subsequent years, by 2007 an extra £3.5 trillion in aid would have flowed to the developing world.

Global environmental leadership

Superpowers and emerging powers have responsibilities in terms of the global environment. The USA, EU, Japan and the BRICs are the world's major resource consumers and polluters. As the world faces significant global warming, it is these countries that must bear the brunt of the changes in consumption patterns that are needed to reduce greenhouse gas emissions. So far their record has been mixed:

■ A landmark international agreement on reducing ozone-depleting CFCs was reached in 1987 — the Montreal Protocol. This seemed to suggest that the most powerful nations could work together to solve global environmental issues. The Protocol was described by former UN Secretary General Kofi Annan as 'perhaps the single most successful international agreement to date'.

■ This good start was followed by the Earth Summit in Rio de Janeiro in 1992 (The UN Conference on Environment and Development) which raised environmental issues onto the global agenda.

■ In 1997, the Kyoto Protocol was on the table. This was the first attempt to reduce greenhouse gas emissions among developed nations. Reaching agreement proved much harder than 10 years earlier in Montreal. The USA refused to sign the Kyoto agreement, as did Russia and Australia (both of whom later signed up); Canada initially signed, then withdrew.

■ The failure to reach universal agreement at Kyoto was significant. Ten years later at the Bali Summit disagreement surfaced once more, particularly between the EU and USA. Bali was a prelude to a summit in Copenhagen in 2009, which aims to create a 'Son of Kyoto' treaty to cut greenhouse gas emissions. Crucially, this will attempt to involve the BRICs in cuts. It remains to be seen whether an agreement can be reached.

On a more positive note, the EU has shown that systems can be put in place to help reduce emissions. In 2005, the EU began a carbon trading system called EU ETS (European Union Emission Trading Scheme). It is the world's only compulsory example of a 'cap-and-trade' system, covering around 50% of all EU carbon emissions. The power generation, steel, cement and other large heavily polluting industries are currently part of the scheme. The ETS has experienced problems but it may form a model for similar schemes in the USA and perhaps worldwide.

Sustainable superpowers?

The Brundtland Commission (1987) definition of sustainable development stated that development should 'meet the needs of the present without compromising the ability of future generations to meet their own needs'. Can the existing superpowers and emerging powers be sustainable? Much of the evidence that has been examined suggests that they cannot. It is clear that from an environmental and ecological perspective, the Earth can barely cope with the demands of the current superpowers. A future in which the BRICs grow to similar levels of development and power as the USA and EU today is in many ways unthinkable. On the other hand, it is clear that development is needed in India and China where many people still live in poverty. Rather than attempt to argue in great detail how an individual country can meet the demands of sustainable development, it may be more useful to examine some global strategies that superpowers and emerging powers might aim for:

■ a workable agreement on greenhouse gas emissions to replace Kyoto from 2012. This must involve the BRICs as well as the EU, USA and Japan, i.e. almost 75% of the world's current greenhouse gas emissions.

■ a commitment to work towards meeting the 0.7% of GNP aid target first agreed in 1970. This additional aid could help overcome increasing global inequality as well as some of it being used to help developing nations adapt to the inevitable climate changes of the twenty-first century.

■ renewal of the Antarctic Treaty and a commitment to work with the UN to draw up a similar agreement to govern the non-territorial Arctic. Without these, it is likely that increasing pressure for natural resources will lead to degradation of both locations.

■ a commitment from the superpowers and emerging powers to operate within international trade norms, rather than signing bilateral agreements with developing nations which cede control of their land and mineral resources to a foreign country. This would go some way to ending the neocolonial control of developing countries by the rich and powerful.

- a commitment to share developing technologies in the field of renewable energy in order to develop alternatives to fossil fuels rapidly. This would help reduce dependency on fossil fuels and would provide an alternative path for development in the BRICs.
- a commitment to change the membership of key international organisations by allowing some, or all, the BRIC countries to join. This would make international decision making more representative of the world population as a whole.

It is clear that the closing years of the first decade of the twenty-first century are a time of transition from a unipolar world order to a multipolar one. It is equally clear that this presents a unique set of global challenges at a time when resources are under unprecedented pressures and the planet's health hangs in the balance.

20

Using case studies

Question

(a) **Compare and contrast the Arctic and Antarctic in terms of the threats they face and their management.**

(b) **To what extent do the current superpowers and emerging powers demonstrate social and environmental leadership?**

Guidance

(a) Look for similarities and differences between the Arctic and Antarctic. Both face the threat of resources exploitation, although the threat is more immediate in the Arctic. There is a key contrast between a managed Antarctic (the Antarctic Treaty) and an 'open' Arctic. Lack of any Arctic agreement might itself be seen as a major threat to the area's wilderness status.

(b) You must take care to be balanced when answering this question. Many students would approach it by being very anti-American because of that nation's refusal to sign the Kyoto agreement and the low percentage of GNP it gives as aid. Of course, the USA is the largest giver of aid in raw dollar terms. Remember that there have been successes, such as the Montreal Protocol and the EU ETS.

Examination advice

The golden rules for success

In the heat of the exam, it is easy to forget the golden rules of doing well in geography exams. These apply particularly at A2, because questions are more open and less structured and you are 'on you own' more than at AS. Try to remember these rules:

- **Range** Try to give several examples — at least two. If the question allows for it, try to make the examples a bit different (contrasting), such as one at a large scale and one at a small scale.
- **Balance** If you are discussing a topic or issues, try to give both sides of the argument — for example, 'costs and benefits' or 'advantages and disadvantages'. Don't be one-sided.
- **Facts** Try to include some hard facts. It is much better to say '$3.5 billion' rather than 'lots of money'.
- **Style** Avoid writing in the first person. Try not to write 'I think that…' or 'My conclusion is…'. Instead, use the third person, e.g. 'A common view is…' or 'Overall, the evidence suggests that…'.
- **Place** Geography is about places. An exam answer that does not refer to any places will be weak. When you use examples, name them and say where they are.
- **Structure** Rather than just writing and writing, try to write to a structure. When writing about impacts, commonly used examples are social, economic and environmental positives and negatives. Costs and benefits to host and source is a useful structure when writing about movement (people, industry or money).
- **Relevance** You should be careful about information sources and data. Try to make sure that you are using up-to-date information. China and India are rapidly changing, so relying on information from the 1990s is likely to paint only a partial picture.
- **Realism** Be careful how you phrase things. Here are some (common) simplistic statements that could make your answer look less than convincing:
  - 'the country of Africa' — you mean continent
  - 'in the developing world there is no education' —there is education, it is just not well funded and the number of years in school is often low
  - 'South Korea, an LEDC country' — you mean NIC
  - 'most migrants to the UK live off social security' — a tabloid headline, which is simply not true

None of the above statements in true. Do not fall into the trap of making sweeping statements. They are likely to be wrong.

■ **Overview** Even if you are not asked to in the question, you should try to provide an overview at the end of your answer. All you need are perhaps two sentences that summarise what you have said and 'round off' your answer. Examiners are impressed by this.

Data stimulus

You are very likely to be asked to use resources in many of your AS and A2 exams. The topics covered in this book are global in nature and this makes it likely that you will encounter particular types of resources. You will be asked to analyse, describe and explain these. Some resources prove particularly problematic and these are considered here.

World maps

Figure 9.1
The digital access index, 2003

Figure 9.1 shows the digital access index for 2003. It measures how well-connected countries are in terms of telephone lines, mobile phones, internet access and infrastructure as well as education. In an exam you could be asked to describe or analyse the pattern show in Figure 9.1. A question such as this demands a careful, structured approach.

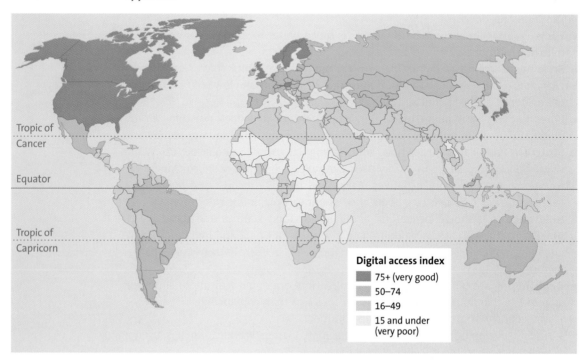

- Read the figure title carefully and note the date — 2003 is reasonably recent, but mobile and internet technology is changing fast. Read the key carefully; it is easy to misread the colour shading values.
- Look for patterns. Very few world maps display a stark, simplistic North–South divide and this map is no exception. Central Africa has very low values, but northern and southern Africa are in the 16–49 band. Note that parts of South America have similar values to much of Europe. Europe itself does not have universally high values.
- Look for anomalies. In this case, Laos stands out in Asia as having a very low value and the value for Malaysia is higher than surrounding areas. The UAE is a high anomaly in the Middle East.

Tables of data

Tables of statistics tend to put candidates off questions. There is no reason to fear them. A good tip is to take a highlighter pen into the exam and, if you encounter a table, be prepared to use it. A typical example is shown in Table 9.1.

Table 9.1
The BRICs compared

Data source, Goldman Sachs, 2007 and WRI	Total economic growth 2000–07	Internet use growth 2000–08	Additional years life expectancy added between 2000 and 2005	$ GDP per capita, 2007	$ GDP per capita, 2050	Additional population 2007–50
Russia	185%	1024%	+1.0	9000	78 000	−30 million
Brazil	104%	900%	+1.4	7000	50 000	130 million
China	397%	950%	+0.7	2500	50 000	150 million
India	144%	1100%	+1.8	1000	21 000	500 million

- Read the title carefully. In this case, the focus is on the four BRIC countries.
- As with maps, look for a date. This table contains a range of data from different dates ranging from the period 2000–05 and projections to 2050. Some of the data are fairly contemporary and are likely to be reliable, but the projections are much less secure.
- Pick out patterns with your highlighter. Notice that some of the data are similar for all four countries, e.g. internet use growth 2000–2008, whereas total economic growth has a much larger range.
- Some data are paired; for instance in terms of GDP per capita in 2007 there are two well-off countries (Russia and Brazil) and two poorer ones (China and India).
- Look for obvious anomalies. Russia's projected population decline is probably the clearest of these. India's projected GDP per capita in 2050 is much lower than that of the other three countries.

Graphs

Like tables, graphs can be off-putting and may appear initially to be very complicated. You should expect more complex graphs at A2, compared with AS. They may show several types of data together, or compare different countries, as in Figure 9.2.

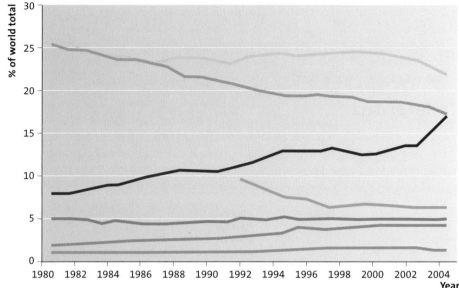

Figure 9.2
Trends in carbon dioxide emissions

- Take careful note of the labels on axes. In this case, time is on the *x*-axis and carbon dioxide as a percentage of world total emissions is on the *y*-axis.
- Note the key. Seven countries/regions are shown here. Note that the data for Russia only go back to 1992. This is because before this data 'Russia' did not exist; it was part of the USSR.
- Look for general patterns first. Four of the lines are towards the bottom of the graph, whereas China, Europe and the USA are towards the top. This suggests a difference between these groups.
- Look for trends. Europe and the USA have a sharply falling share whereas China's share is rising — dramatically in the period 2002–04. Other countries are reasonably stable.
- Look for anomalies. The line for Russia declines between 1992 and 1998 but has since stabilised.

Using case studies

A common problem in examinations is using case studies, but not *actually* using case studies. Candidates often name their case study — for example, 'China' — but then fail to deliver. The most common reason is that very little information that is *specific* to China is presented. You need to be careful that your answer does not read as if it could apply to any BRIC.

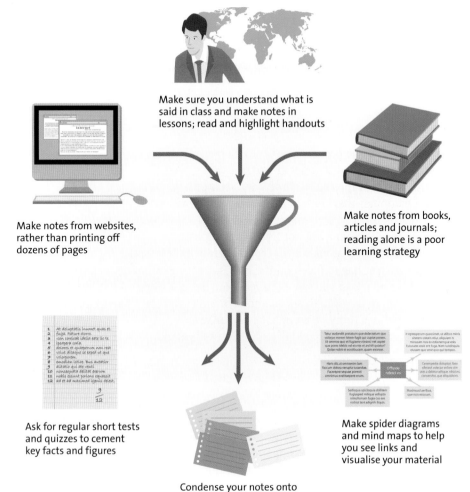

Make sure you understand what is said in class and make notes in lessons; read and highlight handouts

Make notes from websites, rather than printing off dozens of pages

Make notes from books, articles and journals; reading alone is a poor learning strategy

Ask for regular short tests and quizzes to cement key facts and figures

Make spider diagrams and mind maps to help you see links and visualise your material

Condense your notes onto flash cards during revision

Figure 9.3
Processing and condensing information

Lack of detailed case study knowledge comes down largely to revision. However, the process of *not* having enough detailed knowledge to make a strong case in the exam begins earlier. Figure 9.3 gives some tips on how to ensure that you use your case studies successfully. The trick is to *use* information rather than just gathering it. You should condense it into a form that is easy to revise from.

In the exam, remember that a single case study is only likely to prove one or two points. Well-written answers are usually comparative and supported. This means that:

- case studies should be backed up by smaller supporting examples, which help to reinforce the point you are making
- case studies and examples should be compared to draw out their differences

Using case studies and examples in this way makes exam responses more discursive — in other words, it will help you build up an argument rather than just writing a description.

Understanding questions

Exam questions follow a standard structure that you need to understand. Here is an example:

'Using examples, evaluate the social and economic costs and benefits of rapid economic development in the BRICs.'

This question can be broken down into three types of word:

- **Instruction words** tell you that you must:
  - use examples (probably named and located ones)
  - use examples that contain both costs and benefits
- **Key words** form a 'box' that sets the boundaries for your answer. If you stray outside this box, you will not be answering the question. Key words outline the detailed content that your answer must cover. In this case:
  - your answer has to focus on the BRICs. Drifting into a discussion of the EU or USA would mean you have strayed from the question.
  - you need to cover both social and economic aspects. Dealing with only one or the other will produce an unbalanced answer.
  - you should focus on rapid economic development

The **command word(s)** tells you how to approach writing your answer. In this case it is 'evaluate'. In other words, weigh-up the costs and benefits and make a judgement. Be aware that there could be two or more command words.

The command words used in A2 examination questions are often different from those used at AS and this is perhaps the key difference between AS and A2. It means that you will need to 'raise your game' to continue your success from AS. Table 9.2 shows a simple comparison between AS and A2 command words:

Table 9.2
Commonly used AS and A2 command words

Familiar command words from AS	Moving up to A2
State	Compare
Describe	Explain
Comment on	Assess
Explain	Evaluate
Suggest reasons	Justify

Being synoptic

Synopticity usually forms part of the A2 assessment in geography. It means being able to see 'the big picture'. In class, you usually investigate topics in a linear order. You may study China, then move onto India and perhaps later examine different models that help explain economic growth or superpower relations. This allows you to develop a detailed understanding of each topic in turn. To develop this into 'being synoptic' you need to start to see the links between the separate topics.

Synopticity can be taken further. Links may be developed from topics covered at AS, your A2 options, or even with the other subjects you are studying. Figure 9.4 shows how these wider linkages might be developed.

Synopticity can also be approached by the use of comparative and parallel examples. The aim is to examine an issue by comparing it with other, similar issues. For instance, if a question is about China there may be a place for making a brief comparison with India to help show the particular geographical characteristics of China, i.e. what makes it a special case. Do this with care, as you will need to ensure the bulk of your answer remains rooted in the question asked.

Figure 9.4
Synoptic China

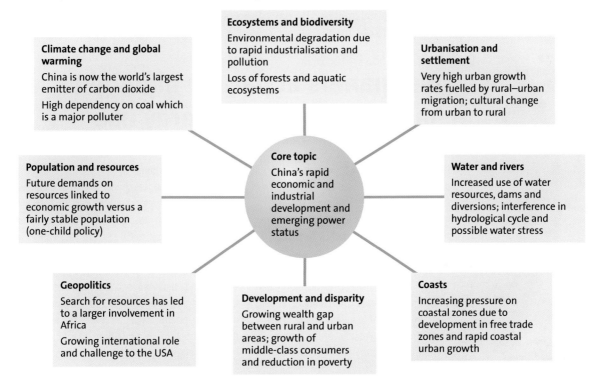

Ecosystems and biodiversity
Environmental degradation due to rapid industrialisation and pollution
Loss of forests and aquatic ecosystems

Climate change and global warming
China is now the world's largest emitter of carbon dioxide
High dependency on coal which is a major polluter

Urbanisation and settlement
Very high urban growth rates fuelled by rural–urban migration; cultural change from urban to rural

Core topic
China's rapid economic and industrial development and emerging power status

Population and resources
Future demands on resources linked to economic growth versus a fairly stable population (one-child policy)

Water and rivers
Increased use of water resources, dams and diversions; interference in hydrological cycle and possible water stress

Geopolitics
Search for resources has led to a larger involvement in Africa
Growing international role and challenge to the USA

Development and disparity
Growing wealth gap between rural and urban areas; growth of middle-class consumers and reduction in poverty

Coasts
Increasing pressure on coastal zones due to development in free trade zones and rapid coastal urban growth

Recognising and avoiding bias

Many of the topics covered in AS and A2 geography are controversial. Superpowers is especially so because it is highly political. People's perceptions of the USSR are a good example. As a communist country, many view the USSR as a failed political and economic experiment whose collapse in the early 1990s was inevitable. They would cite the collapse as evidence that countries that are not democratic and restrict private wealth generation are doomed to fail. Others might argue that the communist USSR promoted universal, good-quality health care and education and satisfied the needs of the majority of its population very well, and should therefore be viewed as a success. There is no right answer here. Your own view depends on your own personal beliefs and values.

Most, if not all, written material about the superpowers and geopolitics is biased in some way. This means that it is selective in the information it chooses to include and leave out and this steers the reader towards a particular view.

Bias is very different from lying or making things up. Even in a heavily biased, one-sided article, all the factual information can be true. The problem is that much relevant information will have been left out, so the article only gives one side of the story.

The article in Figure 9.5 is from **www.chinadaily.com.cn**. *China Daily* is a state-owned, English language newspaper in China, which has a print and web version. The article was published on the day of the 60th anniversary of the founding of the People's Republic of China.

Figure 9.5
China Daily *article*

Solar panels at parade highlight changes in China's energy use

China Daily website, 1 October 2009

Solar panels held by a formation of energy workers at the National Day parade on Thursday demonstrated China's determination to shift to renewable energy in handling climate change. Surrounded by energy workers, a float carrying the sculptures of windmills and oil reserve containers, as well as a banner reading "Striving to develop clean energy" moving past Tian'anmen Square at the magnificent pageant marking New China's 60th anniversary of founding. As the world's top energy producer and second largest consumer, it takes several decades for China to rely on its own energy supply to power the double-digit growth of the world's third largest economy. China is the world's top coal maker and the fifth largest crude oil producer. As the global efforts on cutting greenhouse gas emissions has never been so urgent, China realized that to solely rely on fossil fuel will hardly sustain its rocketing economic growth. On Sept 22, President Hu promised at the United Nations General Assembly to vigorously develop renewable energy and nuclear energy, and to increase the share of non-fossil fuels in primary energy use to around 15 percent by 2020. Over the past decades, changes have already taken place. Of the total energy use, China's coal consumption has been lowered from 96 percent in 1952 to 68 percent last year. The use of hydro, nuclear and wind power was raised from 1.61 percent to 9.5 percent. The nation boasts Asia's biggest wind power turbine engine, and some 9,100 megawatts of nuclear energy capacity. It has approved the construction of additional reactors to increase output to 32,000 megawatts. To save fuel, China's pioneering automaker BYD began selling the world's first plug-in hybrid vehicle in December last year and plans to make it to the European and North American markets. Official data showed China cut its energy consumption per unit of GDP by 10.1 percent from 2006 to 2008, which means it saved 300 million tons of standard coal and cut carbon dioxide emissions by 750 million tons. China reported a drop of 3.35 percent of energy consumption per unit of GDP in the first half of this year from the same period a year ago, laying the foundations for a 20 percent cut by 2010 from the level in 2005.

Read the article and consider the impression it gives of China's energy sector.

Much attention in given to renewable energy (in yellow), which might give the impression that China gets much of its electricity from renewable sources — in fact only around 16% of electricity was renewable in 2006.

The article uses words such as 'cut' and 'drop' (green) to, perhaps, give the impression that energy use and carbon emissions are falling. This is not the case. Reading carefully, it become clear that, for instance, energy consumption per unit of GDP is falling, but as GDP is growing, total energy use is growing also.

You might be forgiven for thinking that coal consumption in China has fallen, as the article says: 'China's coal consumption has been lowered from 96 percent in 1952 to 68 percent last year'. In fact total coal use in China rose by close to 7% in 2008 alone, to 1.4 billion tonnes of oil equivalent; only the proportion of total energy coming from coal fell between 1952 and 2008.

None of the facts in the article is incorrect, but it could be argued that they are used to give the impression of a 'green' China, reducing its emissions and coal consumption.

When you are reading and researching material you need to be aware that many sources will be biased. Try to avoid heavily biased material and spot the more subtle forms by:

- researching well known magazines, articles and journals. These will tend to be less biased, especially if they are peer reviewed.
- being aware that some common sources are well-known for having a particular viewpoint and set of values, e.g. daily newspapers. As long as you know what these perspectives are, bias becomes easier to spot.
- being wary of the internet. Some sites are very well maintained and balanced, others less so. Try to locate the 'about us' page and find out who funds the website and contributes to it.
- asking a friend or your teacher to read the material and see what he/she thinks

Index

Contemporary Case Studies